The Avignon Papacy
1305–1403

Bust of Urban V
(*Musée Calvet, Avignon*)

The
Avignon Papacy
1305-1403

by
YVES RENOUARD

translated by
DENIS BETHELL

ARCHON BOOKS
1970

This edition first published
in the United States by Archon Books 1970
Hamden, Connecticut
Printed in Great Britain by
Latimer Trend & Co Ltd Plymouth
All rights reserved

ISBN 0–208–01156–0

Originally published by
Presses Universitaires de France, Paris,
as
La Papauté à Avignon

Contents

Illustrations

Bust of Urban V (*Musée Calvet, Avignon*) (*frontispiece*)

Maps:

Translator's Foreword

Professor Yves Renouard was born at Paris in 1908, and died there on January 15th, 1965. He was without doubt one of the leading French medievalists of his time, and was particularly expert in the history of Southern France, the Italian cities, and the Avignon papacy. An obituary of him by Professor Charles Edmond Perrin will be found in the *Revue Historique*, vol. 234 (1965), pp. 261-7. Professor Perrin has recently produced a very full collection of his papers (Yves Renouard, *Etudes d'histoire mediévale*, Bibliothêque de l'École Pratique des Hautes Etudes, VIe. section, S.E.P.E.N., Paris, 1968). His short book on the Avignon papacy published in the 'Que Sais—Je?' series in 1954 and here translated, is a brilliant summary of a lifetime's research and the best brief introduction to the subject there is.

For the benefit of English-speaking readers, the translation has been given an additional bibliography consisting mainly of works in English, an appendix listing the popes between 1288 and 1431, some maps, and a number of explanatory footnotes. The aim throughout has been to give as clear as possible a rendering of what Professor Renouard has said. A few explanatory phrases and sentences have also been added in the text to help fill out the historical and geographical background. On three occasions where I disagree with Professor Renouard's views I have ventured to give a footnote referring to books where a different interpretation will be found. I have, for purposes of greater clarity, given the names of the Avignon antipopes in inverted commas (see the appendix), and used inverted commas in a number of other places where it has seemed to me possible that an English reader unfamiliar with the period might be confused: for example, in speaking of the French kingdom of Sicily, which did not in the fourteenth century include Sicily. It has not always been possible to convey Professor Renouard's style. This translation is the work of a teacher of medieval history anxious to give pupils who do not read French the benefit of what Renouard wrote. As such, I hope it will be accepted as a tribute to him, and encourage them to learn French and read his work for themselves.

I am grateful to Dr. Michael Clanchy who first introduced me to the subject with a fascinating lecture on the building of the papal palace at Avignon, and lent me Professor Renouard's book; to Mrs. Janet Morgan who went over the translation with great care to eliminate mistakes; and to Mrs. Anne Morgenstern who gave useful advice on the bibliography.

Introduction

On September 7th, 1303, Guillaume de Nogaret entered the Italian town of Anagni by force with the help of the troops of the Colonna family. The King of France, Philip the Fair, had sent him to tell Pope Boniface VIII that he, the King of France, was citing him, the pope, before a General Council. The pope was captured, imprisoned, insulted, perhaps even struck. The people of Anagni rose to deliver him, but none the less he died of shock and exhaustion on October 20th, 1303.

This incident at Anagni and Boniface's subsequent death together mark the onset of a new epoch of Church history at the beginning of the fourteenth century. The break with the previous period becomes more marked and significant when one thinks of the events which led up to these. In 1291 the Saracens had captured Acre and had put a final end to the crusading states in the Holy Land. On July 5th, 1294, the hermit, Peter of Morrone, had been elected pope as Celestine V, and this election showed how much Franciscan ideas of a reformed and spiritualised Church had affected public opinion. On December 13th, 1294, Celestine had resigned. For a pope to resign was unprecedented, and his resignation emphasised first what a vast burden it was to administer the Church, second that idealism and candour were not enough to qualify a man to administer it, and third the power of the college of cardinals. The discussions which followed showed how uncertain papal rights and powers still were. When Philip summoned Boniface to come before a General Council on a charge of heresy the whole structure of the Church was being questioned. The idea of the summons came from Philip's lawyers, a fact which showed the rise of a new educated lay opinion, of laymen with views they could express on Church affairs. It demonstrated, too, that heresy might be stifled but that doctrinal problems remained. The brutal attack on Anagni by the Colonna, and the assault on the Pope himself while he was staying with his own family, the Gaetani, showed that the faction fights of the Roman nobility, and of the papal states generally, had reached what was virtually a state of civil war. Finally, Boniface's death before he had published his bull excommunicating Philip demonstrated the strength of the national kings as compared with that of the head of Christendom.

This series of events, at once important in themselves and dramatic in their consequences, makes much more understandable the collapse of the system which successive popes had built up since the Gregorian reform of the eleventh century. That system had grown up and been consolidated alongside the great crusading movement. Pope Urban II had proclaimed the first crusade of 1099, and its success had placed the pope at the head of Western Christendom and made public opinion receptive to papal leadership. Partly in consequence the twelfth century had seen the fulfilment of Gregory VII's ideas of moral and administrative reform, with papal influence on every aspect of Christian life and papal interference, by means of papal legates, in every province and corner of Christendom. The crusade helped the centralization of the Church under papal authority. The popes had laid crusading tithes on all ecclesiastical benefices and established a general system of taxation. They had intervened in government for moral reasons and asserted their right to depose emperors and kings. Christian Europe had been feudally united to the papacy when Western kings had sworn oaths of vassalage to the popes. Through the universities of the thirteenth century the popes had been able to control and expand dogma, and through the new orders of mendicant friars, settled in the towns, with their centralized command in a Master General (usually at the pope's side), the popes could control the spiritual lives of the common people.

Introduction

But there was much in Western civilization which accorded very ill with all this, as indeed the events of the 1290s made clear. For the papacy the solution could only be reaction or change. Boniface's solution was a new crusade. Political success would support doctrinal reaction. But the national kings had become too strong to allow their vassals to enlist without permission for a crusade even if they had wanted to, and the kings of France and England were too preoccupied by their quarrel in Aquitaine to be prepared to go East. Under the circumstances the pope's theocratic pretensions were singularly ill timed. The declaration of Boniface's bull *Unam Sanctam*, 'Every human creature is subject to the Roman pontiff' (November 18th, 1302), was soon seen as an empty and irritating formula. French public opinion supported Philip the Fair in his unprecedented attack on papal pretensions which led up to the violent scene at Anagni.

There could be no going back. If the Church was to continue to perform its mission there had to be a transformation of its life and organization in Western society. Such adaptions are frequent enough in the history of institutions which, like the Church, span many centuries and undergo constant renewal. Each such adaptation has a special character of its own.

The special feature of this fourteenth-century reorganization was that it took place not at Rome, nor in the papal states in Italy, but at Avignon where the popes stayed established from 1309 to 1376. The popes of this period were Frenchmen, and they were at Avignon during the Hundred Years War between England and France. Their nationality and their place of residence certainly influenced their solutions of the Church's problems and the way in which they adapted its traditional role to day-to-day events and the general development of Western civilization. The period which opened after the pontificate of the shortlived Benedict XI (1303–4) has thus a strongly marked and highly original character: it is the only period in which the popes have regularly lived in one stable residence outside Rome and away from the tomb of St. Peter. This stay at Avignon laid a special imprint on the ways in which the fourteenth-century popes tried to adapt the Church and Christian society to new conditions by new solutions and changes. The influence of their stay at Avignon on the destinies of Christendom is the subject of this book.

I

The Papacy Settles at Avignon, 1305–16

The Roman nobility were divided between the factions of the Gaetani and the Colonna, and their fights made Rome and the countryside round it, the Campagna, wretchedly unsafe. Benedict XI like many of his predecessors decided to seek safety elsewhere in the papal states.

The papal states were those lands where the pope was sovereign (except in the difficult constitutional situation when the Holy Roman Emperor was actually present in them) and which the pope governed either directly or through legates. Outside Rome there were eight papal provinces: the Romagna; the town and county of Bologna; the March of Ancona; the Duchy of Spoleto; the Patrimony of St. Peter in Tuscany; the Campagna and Marittima; the town and territory of Bene-vento; and, beyond the Alps, the Comtat Venaissin in Provence. The Italian provinces together made up a Papal State which cut across the centre of Italy from Ancona to Terracina, and it was almost at the dead centre of Italy, at Perugia, one of the most important towns of the Duchy of Spoleto, that Benedict XI took up his residence in March, 1304 and died on July 17th of that same year.

The conclave of cardinals to elect a new pope consequently met at Perugia. It had an important and difficult decision to make. Benedict XI had been elected by the conclave of 1303 with ease for two reasons: one was that he was not a Roman, the other that his absence from the curia during the great quarrel between Boniface VIII and Philip the Fair made him the sole neutral cardinal. It had been his task to heal the conflict. He had done his best in the short time given him by dissociating the King of France from his counsellors and pardoning Philip the Fair, while condemning Nogaret, the Colonna, and the principal offenders at Anagni. But Philip continued to rely on Nogaret and demanded the summoning of a General Council to judge Boniface's acts and teaching. Benedict had not replied to that demand; but an answer had to be given—an answer that would, in effect, be given when the conclave elected a new pope.

There were no more neutral cardinals: the college was divided —either for or against Boniface and his policies—and the division was sharpened by the family politics of Rome. It was too sharp for the necessary two-thirds majority of votes to be found for any candidate, and the conclave dragged on for months while the kings and princes of Europe tried to put pressure on it, especially Philip.

At length, when it was plain that no one of the cardinals would ever obtain the votes of his brethren, it was decided to look outside the college for some prelate who would take an impartial view of Boniface and his policies. Bertrand de Got, archbishop of Bordeaux, was a famous canon lawyer. His name was mentioned and received favourably, and he was elected pope on June 5th, 1305.

Bertrand de Got was a subject of the king of France, and his election could be taken as a gesture of appeasement to Philip; but as archbishop of Bordeaux he was a vassal of the Duke of Aquitaine, Edward I of England. He had not been appointed to his see by Philip, and, although forbidden to do so by Philip, he had attended the Council summoned by Boniface at Rome in 1302. He had shown his independence; he was known as a peacemaker. It was known as well that he was on good terms with both Edward and Philip, and he seemed to be the ideal man to make peace between them in Aquitaine, and to turn their attention to a crusade in the East.

He was not a cardinal, and consequently not at Perugia when he was elected. The news reached him at Lusignan in Poitou where he was in process of making an archiepiscopal visitation

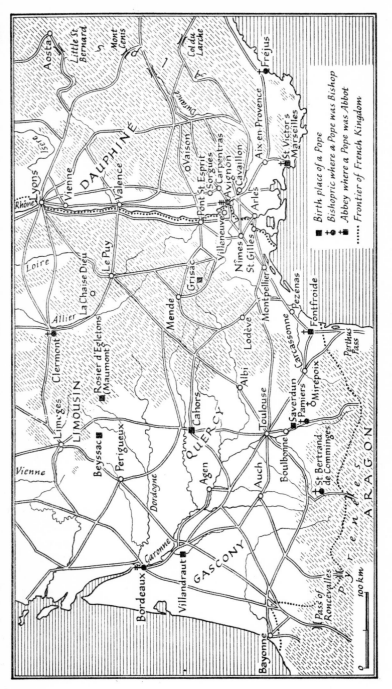

THE LANGUE D'OC (after B. Guillemain, *La Cour Pontificale d'Avignon*)

of his province. That was on June 19th, 1305. He decided to take the name Clement V and set out for Italy, intending to be crowned at Vienne, on the Rhône, then in the Holy Roman Empire, where princes and prelates from all over Christendom could attend the coronation. Philip the Fair persuaded him instead to choose Lyons, part of which (the part on the right bank of the Saône) was in France, and there, in Philip's presence, Clement V was crowned on November 14th, 1305. Edward I had been unable to come because of the war in Scotland. This was a pity, for Clement was a Gascon with a fervent love for his native country, Aquitaine, and his interview with Philip reinforced his determination to settle the disagreement between France and England over it. Meanwhile, the cardinals from Perugia confirmed the bad news of disorders in Italy and the papal state. Clement gladly decided to stay in France and carry out his most immediate wish—to do what he could for Aquitaine.

It was thus in his first weeks as pope that Clement, without realizing that he was doing anything of the sort, determined the papacy's long stay in the Rhône valley. Not that his heart lay *there*. He loved Gascony, where he had been born; his career had been made at Agen, St. Bertrand de Comminges, and at Bordeaux. He surrounded himself with Gascons, and at once created ten Gascon cardinals. His Gascon entourage and his shaky health both made him think of home. So did his desire to solve the Aquitaine problem, from personal involvement, as friend and subject of both the kings concerned, and from general policy, since he knew that peace in Aquitaine was essential for any successful crusade. Moreover, from 1305 on, there was a constant succession of problems and issues of major importance raised with Clement by Philip, which prevented him from setting out for Italy. In 1306 a severe illness kept Clement at Bordeaux, and this meant that he was able to have no second meeting with Philip till May, 1307, when they met at Poitiers. Very shortly after there broke out the whole business of the trial of the knights Templar. Philip announced his discovery of all sorts of doctrinal and moral evils among the Templars and his intention to punish them. Public opinion, shaken and disturbed by the final abandonment of the Holy Land, seemed disposed to believe him, and pleased to have a scapegoat. Clement stayed in south-west France to negotiate; fresh problems kept arising; his attempt to protect the Templars led to fresh attacks by Philip on Boniface's memory, and in 1308 they had a third interview, again at Poitiers. The only answer to the Templar question seemed to be a General Council, and on August 12th, 1308, Clement summoned a Council to meet on October 1st, 1310, at Vienne.

Thus it was that after his election Clement stayed in the south of France, from 1307 onwards gathering more and more of the curia around him. Naturally, once he had decided on the Council at Vienne, it was only sensible to wait for the Council, either at Vienne, or in its neighbourhood. Aquitaine was too much on the edge of things. The accession of Edward II in 1307, and his marriage (which Clement had helped to bring about) with Isabella of France, had brought a temporary end to trouble over Aquitaine in any case. Finally, Aquitaine was part of France and Clement wanted to be out of France and independent of Philip—though near enough to continue negotiations. He wanted as well to be nearer to Germany, where he was trying skilfully to bring about the election of Henry of Luxemburg as 'King of the Romans', and to frustrate Philip's aims for that position. He needed to be nearer to Italy, where Henry would come to be crowned as Holy Roman Emperor, and where war was raging between Venice and the pope over the succession to Ferrara (papal territory held feudally from the Holy See where Clement was now vainly trying to re-establish his direct rule and authority). In Vienne itself there were all the problems to be solved of the housing and feeding of an oecumenical council.

The Comtat Venaissin was near Vienne, near France, near Germany and near Italy, and it was the only papal territory on the French side of the Alps.

The Comtat Venaissin was a number of fiefs held from the pope by homage and sixty or so castles and villages held by him directly, all between the rivers Aygues and Durance, on the left bank of the Rhône, in the ancient kingdom of Arles, which formed part of the Holy Roman Empire. In 1229 Raymond VII, Count of Toulouse, had ceded it to the pope, but no pope had taken possession of it till 1274, some years after the death of Alphonse of Poitiers (St. Louis's brother, and Philip the Fair's great-uncle) and that of his wife, Jeanne of Toulouse, Raymond's heiress. Its principal towns were Carpentras and Cavaillon, each held of the pope in fief by their bishops, and Pernes and Vaison, both directly governed by the pope, the first being the centre of his administration, while the other was the cathedral city.

There was nothing extraordinary about the pope's taking up residence there on the eve of the Council. It was papal land and suited his needs admirably. But in fact Clement did not go to any of the four little principal towns of the Comtat Venaissin, but settled at the western edge of the county, at Avignon, which since 1290 had belonged to Charles II 'King of Sicily' in his capacity as count of Provence and French prince.[1] It seems likely that Clement's choice was determined by the importance of the town, with its new university and its site on the Rhône which made it easily accessible from north and south and from Vienne. An added attraction, perhaps, was the protection which could be afforded by King Charles of 'Sicily'. When, on April 4th, 1310, Clement V postponed the Council till October 1st, 1311, he prolonged his stay; and there is nothing more surprising about his two-year residence at Avignon in the town of his vassal King Charles (who held his Italian lands from the pope) than there is about his two previous

[1] Pope Urban IV invited Charles of Anjou, St. Louis's brother, to conquer the papal fief of Southern Italy and Sicily in 1265. He did so, but in 1282 the Sicilians revolted against French domination, and called on the king of Aragon to become their king. Thenceforward there were two kings of Sicily, the Aragonese king who actually ruled Sicily from Palermo, and who was sometimes referred to as king of 'Trinacria', and the French king of the house of Anjou, who ruled southern Italy from Naples, and who was called 'King of Sicily' without being able to reconquer it. The two were usually at war. The long duration of this situation explains the curious expression 'the Kingdom of the Two Sicilies' when the two were eventually reunited.

(Translator's note.)

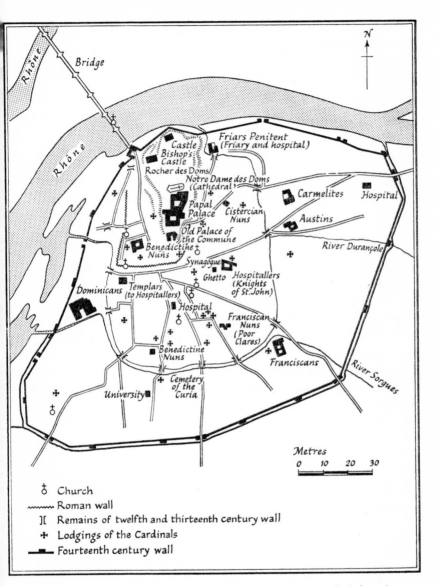

N

Bridge

Rhône

Rhône

Castle
Bishop's
Castle
Rocher des Doms

Friars Penitent
(Friary and hospital)

Notre Dame des Doms
(Cathedral)

Carmelites

Hospital

Papal
Palace

Cistercian
Nuns

Austins

Old Palace of
the Commune

River Durançole

Benedictine
Nuns

Synagogue

Ghetto

Hospitallers
(Knights
of St. John)

Dominicans

Templars
(to Hospitallers)

Hospital

Franciscan
Nuns
(Poor
Clares)

Benedictine
Nuns

Franciscans

River Sorgues

Cemetery
of the
Curia

University

Metres
0   10   20   30

ồ Church
〜〜〜 Roman wall
][Remains of twelfth and thirteenth century wall
✛ Lodgings of the Cardinals
▬■▬ Fourteenth century wall

Avignon (after B. Guillemain, *La Cour Pontificale d' Avignon*) years of wandering in Southern France. He arrived at Avignon on March 9th, 1309, and put up there in a humble way—not intending a long stay—at the Dominican priory. Each summer he left the hot town for the cooler hills of the Comtat Venaissin, for a couple of months in 1309, for four months in 1311 and for three and a half months in 1312, staying either at the priory of Groseau or at Châteauneuf.

So it was that Clement V made Avignon the residence of the papacy. His stay there is characteristic: he was an intelligent man but a sick one, and his policy in general was clearheaded, subtle and rather weak. His predecessors had left him grave problems both in the world at large, and especially in France and Italy. He could not choose between the brutal alternatives thrust upon him, hesitating between the merits and dangers of decision: he was too conscious of the human and material factors involved. He sought constantly for compromise; and in seeking it sacrificed many of the more radical pretensions of his predecessors. What he sought was a balanced moderation. It was just such a balanced position that Avignon held on the map of Latin Christendom, a half-way house between France and Italy. Rome was nearer the edge of Christendom, more peripheral to it; but Avignon could never be in the fullest sense the proper seat of the papacy.

Once the Council of Vienne was over, in the spring of 1312, Henry VII of Germany marched into Italy. The whole country between Rome and Milan was convulsed, and the papal states were stirred up to even greater disorder and chaos. There could be no question of return to central Italy. Clement therefore spent the summer of 1312 in the Comtat, and then the winter of 1312–13 in Avignon. Meanwhile, one of his nephews bought the castle of Monteux, near Carpentras. Clement was ill and went to stay there with his family, spending the next winter as well in the Comtat, without returning to Avignon. The curia moved to Carpentras. When spring came in 1314 Clement was no better but rather worse. He decided to go home to his native Gascony in search of recovery. But he had barely crossed the Rhône on his way home when he died, at Roquemaure, on

April 6th, 1314. The curia was still at Carpentras when the news came. Clement V had decreed that the conclave must be held either in the diocese where the pope had died or else in the place where the curia was officially resident on the day of his death. The conclave met at Carpentras, in papal territory. That accident might have made Carpentras the papal residence until the popes returned to Rome.

However, a series of further accidents made it improbable. The cardinals were split into factions—Italians, Gascons, Provençals, and seemed unlikely to reach a rapid decision. As a demonstration in favour of their candidate the Gascon cardinals seem to have incited an attack on the conclave by Gascon mercenaries in July, 1314, mercenaries who were in the pay of Clement's family. The only result was that the cardinals broke up the conclave and fled. Some of them took refuge at Avignon under the protection of the king of 'Sicily'—making it clear that Avignon was a safer place than Carpentras. Finally, after long negotiations and under strong pressure from the King of France, the cardinals regathered in conclave at Lyons and with some difficulty elected an elderly pope on August 7th, 1316, Jacques Duèse, who took the name of John XXII.

Now Jacques Duèse, before he became cardinal, had been bishop of Avignon. He knew the bishop's palace on its rock south of the cathedral very well, he was fond of it, and it was easy for him to go back there because his successor was one of his nephews, Jacques de Via. It was familiar, it was convenient, the town was well sited, large, and on one of the most important trade routes of the West. John XXII took the papacy back to Avignon. He took up residence in the bishop's palace. When he created Jacques de Via a cardinal in 1317 he took the bishopric into his own hands rather than inconvenience any new bishop not related to him, and the diocese was administered by the bishop of Marseilles. He went on living comfortably in his old home, waiting for the time when it would be possible to go back to Italy. Administrative logic would have made Carpentras the pope's residence, but the accidents of the Gascon attack on the conclave and John XXII's love for his old bishopric both helped the papacy to settle in Avignon, and once they were there helped popes to realize the advantages of its site. As long as the popes stayed beyond the Alps, Avignon would have the profit and glory of their stay.

II

Avignon as the Temporary Residence of the Papacy, 1316–34

John XXII became pope under much less difficult conditions than his predecessor. The vital questions which had been raised by Boniface VIII and Philip the Fair, where two opposed notions of Christian society had confronted each other in a way which threatened and brought in question the whole structure of the Church, had not been solved, but they had been compromised or lulled by the clever pliability of Clement V. There were plenty of pressing problems as the removal of the conclave to Lyons had shown, but these were more political than theoretical, military and administrative problems which could be dealt with all the more easily since the new energetic pope did not have to face Philip the Fair and his lawyers. John might be an old man of seventy-two; however, unlike Clement he was in good health, uncommonly active and energetic in decision. Whether it was politics, administration, finance or things spiritual, he showed an amazingly clear mind with a quick grasp of essentials and a sense of order. He knew where, when, and how to intervene, logically and practically. He had the vigour to see that his decisions were carried out and respected. He was both planner and executor, an administrator of genius whose mark may even now be seen in several features of the Church's government.

He had been born in Cahors and he surrounded himself with Cahorsin relations and friends. Like Clement he was a nepotist, though his nephews were from Quercy, not Gascony. But if Quercy was his home, it was in Provence that he had made his ecclesiastical career. He had become bishop of Fréjus in 1300, he had been chosen as Chancellor by Charles II of Anjou, count of Provence and king of 'Sicily'. He held a doctorate of civil law as certificate of political and administrative competence. He showed both, and in 1310 became bishop of Avignon.

It was easy and natural for Pope John to reinstall himself at Avignon, but he confined himself to repairing, enlarging and redecorating parts of the episcopal palace. He had no thought of building anything larger, and his building policy makes it quite clear that he thought of Avignon as a purely temporary residence. It seems probable that he had promised (and meant his promise when he made it to the Italian cardinals who had voted for him) that he would return to Italy. He wanted to take the papacy back to Rome.

He could have tried to go. He had the unconditional support of Robert of Anjou, the new count of Provence and king of 'Sicily'. Naples was near Rome and Robert was powerful, as was to be shown when he prevented Henry VII's entrance to the Vatican for his imperial coronation. But Avignon was pleasant to the pope, there was the precedent of Clement V, there were great affairs still unsettled in the West, and Italy and Rome were disturbed and insecure. The news from the papal states was far from reassuring. Most of the cities there had either formed a commune or taken a despot, after the manner of most other Italian cities: either way they had thrown off the control of the rectors of the various papal provinces. This was the moment when the greater communes and more powerful lords in Italy began to build up great territorial states and to do so by drawing the greater towns into their orbits. The cities of the papal states were menaced by powerful neighbours—Ferrara by Venice; Bologna and the towns of the Romagna by the Visconti of Milan; the little towns of the Patrimony of St. Peter by the great Tuscan communes, as was Viterbo by Orvieto, for instance. All this disintegration was furthered by the wretched administration and corruption of the Gascon officials appointed as rectors and treasurers by Clement V. The papal lands were in anarchy and Rome, which had been distracted for fifteen years by the quarrels of the Colonna and the Gaetani, suffered as well from a struggle between a popular party and the nobility. King Robert was the papal vicar in Rome, and the representative of his authority was attacked near the Capitol and hounded out of the city by the popular party. Powerful though Robert might be, it did not seem likely that he could promise the pope peace or dignity in Rome.

John XXII's policy was plain and firm. Order must be re-established in the papal states before he returned to Rome. Naturally he looked for support from the Guelf alliance, the three principal members of which since 1266 had been the pope, the French king of 'Sicily', and the commune of Florence; and equally naturally he resolved to defeat the Ghibelline alliance, whose most important members were the Visconti lords of Milan, the Scaliger lords of Verona, the commune of Pisa and the Aragonese king of 'Trinacria'. The commune of Lucca was shortly to be added to the Ghibelline alliance under a remarkable leader, Castruccio Castracani degli Antelminelli, who dominated Tuscany. The Ghibelline alliance could only be defeated by an army. In 1319, John XXII appointed a fellow Cahorsin whom he had made cardinal, Bertrand du Poujet, to lead the military expedition intended to rescue Northern Italy from the Visconti and Scaligeri and re-establish papal authority in Bologna and the Romagna.

While he waited for his path to be opened to Rome, John XXII concentrated on the problem of the new crusade, as much in the forefront of his mind as in that of Clement V. Clement had persuaded the Council of Vienne to grant a tithe on all ecclesiastical benefices for six years in order to finance a great military and naval expedition for the reconquest of the Holy Land. But if the crusade were to be launched lasting peace had to be made in Aquitaine, for only the united arms of England and France could ensure its success. In Aquitaine the situation worsened despite all the diplomatic efforts of John XXII and a new war broke out there in 1324. After the extinction of the direct Capetian line in France in 1328 and the accession of Philip of Valois as Philip VI—his claim being preferred by the French baronage to that of Edward III of England

—tension mounted even higher. The most Pope John could do was to arm a squadron of ten galleys at Marseilles and Narbonne between 1317 and 1319 and send them to the East as an advance guard for a great expedition for which he worked, dreamed and hoped—but which never sailed.

Moreover, Italian affairs were complicated by events in Germany. The Emperor Henry VII died in 1313. The succession to the Empire was disputed by Frederick of Austria and Lewis of Bavaria. The pope wanted to use the occasion to demonstrate his rights over the Empire, and to decide who was rightful Emperor. In 1322 Lewis beat Frederick at Mühldorf. He decided that Pope John would never recognize him, and crossed the Alps to help Matteo Visconti. Bertrand du Poujet's army had to lift the siege of Milan in 1323 and retire disordered and discomfited. The great expedition against the Visconti had failed.

In the following years Cardinal Bertrand did manage to obtain the submission of a number of towns in Emilia and the Romagna, in particular Bologna, which appointed him as its overlord in 1327. But Lewis of Bavaria's Roman expedition reinforced the Ghibellines throughout Italy and increased (if possible) the disorder and anarchy in Rome itself. On January 17th, 1328, Lewis was crowned Emperor at Rome by the Roman magistrates, on April 14th he declared John XXII deposed for heresy and on May 12th appointed a Franciscan, Peter of Corbara, as pope in John's place with a ludicrous ceremony. In August Lewis was driven out of Rome by the violent reaction he eventually provoked there, and Robert of Naples was called on by the Romans to drive him out. Lewis hurried back to Germany, and in 1330 the Ghibelline league collapsed.

Things looked better for John. True, there was no hope of Rome, where the behaviour of the Romans was not, to say the least, reassuring, but although he was eighty-five John did decide to take the curia to Bologna. Cardinal Bertrand had built a castle in Bologna, the Castello Galliera, to hold the town and keep it in awe. Now he put it in order to receive the pope, who actually intended to move in 1322.

Avignon as the Temporary Residence of the Papacy

It had been John of Bohemia whose intervention in the North of Italy had brought about the restoration of Guelf fortunes and John XXII now thought of a scheme to make a Lombard kingdom in the Po valley—a counterpart to the southern kingdom of Naples, to be held, like the southern kingdom, in vassalage from the Holy See, by John of Bohemia.[1] The idea was very much in the tradition of papal policy in Italy—but it immediately raised the opposition of every city, Guelf or Ghibelline, in the north, each of whom hoped for a share of the wealth of the Po valley, and none of whom wished to see a strong state set up there. The result was a general uprising: John XXII's plans and John of Bohemia's hopes alike crashed to ruin; Cardinal Bertrand du Poujet was chased out of Bologna on March 17th, 1334. When the pope died on December 4th, 1334, his Italian policy was completely shattered, and with it any hope of the return home of the papacy. Such a return would be unlikely, if not impossible in any forseeable future.

★   ★   ★

Despite all John XXII's energetic efforts to take the papacy home, it stayed at Avignon for the eighteen years that he was pope, and it was from Avignon that he conducted both a wide-reaching international diplomacy and the work of reorganizing the Church which, by increasing the papal revenues, would give him the means to reconquer Italy. Steadily these eighteen years showed what an excellent centre Avignon was and how many advantages it had as a centre of Church government.

The first of the advantages, and a great contrast to Rome, was the calm and peace the curia could enjoy there. The population of Avignon was tiny and they neither could nor wanted to disturb the curia whose presence enriched them. The Romans had a thousand-year-old tradition of self government and world government. The Avignonese had no such tradition. It was not in any case against the pope that they had to struggle for any increase in local self government, and the last thing they wanted

[1] Translator's note. For a now commonly held view that John XXII did nothing of the sort, see G. Tabacco, *La Casa di Francia nell' Azione Politica di Papa Giovanni* XXII (Rome, 1953).

to do was to offend their guest. Above everything they wanted him to stay. The bishop's palace was strongly fortified, and, sited as it was on the Rocher des Doms, was in a strong position of natural defence. The king of 'Sicily' was owner of the town as count of Provence, and the pope and cardinals had already appreciated the protection which he could and always would give them.

The second great advantage was Avignon's central position in Christendom which made it an admirable capital (see map iii, p. 33).

Rome owed its greatness and power to its central position in the Mediterranean world of the Roman Empire and early Christianity. But in the early Middle Ages the shape of Christendom had changed. Islam in the seventh and eighth centuries had taken the Middle East, Africa, and much of Spain; the Greek schism had removed the Balkans and Russia. The Latin Empire of Constantinople[1] had collapsed in 1261 and in the early fourteenth century reunion with the Greeks could only be a pious hope. On the other hand the conversion of the Germans, the Scandinavians and the Hungarians had taken the limits of Latin Christendom to Iceland and the Arctic circle, to Prussia and the Carpathians. Fourteenth-century Christendom was no longer the Roman world, and its centre of gravity was northwards. True, the crusade and the East were important preoccupations for the pope and all Christians, but they related to lands which were now far off, exotic, and removed from the main body. The limits of Latin Christianity were Otranto, Cracow, Stockholm, Edinburgh and Lisbon. Rome was 350 miles from Otranto, 700 from Cracow, 1,250 from Stockholm and Edinburgh and 1,100 from Lisbon: in fact, off-centre.

[1] In 1204, the crusaders of the Fourth Crusade had sacked Constantinople, and divided up the Byzantine Empire among French and Italian adventurers. A 'Latin' Emperor—the count of Flanders, was installed in Constantinople and a 'Latin' patriarch in Santa Sophia. The Eastern and Western Churches were thereafter firmly divided with occasional 'unions', accepted by the Greeks for political rather than religious reasons, which were never long lasting. By the late thirteenth century the adventurer states were collapsing before a Greek revival, and before the Turks, who over the next two centuries gradually conquered the Balkans and the Aegean. (Translator's note.)

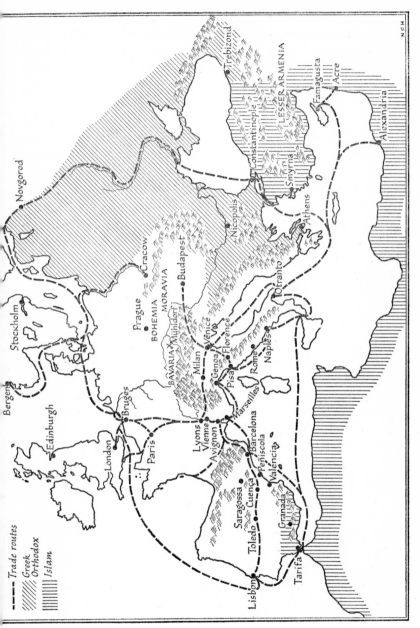

C

Legend:
- – – – Trade routes
- ///// Greek Orthodox
- ≡≡≡ Islam

TRADE ROUTES OF FOURTEENTH-CENTURY EUROPE

Labels on map: Novgorod, Stockholm, Bergen, Edinburgh, London, Paris, Bruges, Prague, BOHEMIA, Cracow, MORAVIA, Budapest, Mühldorf, BAVARIA, Milan, Genoa, Venice, Florence, Pisa, Rome, Naples, Lyons, Vienne, Avignon, Marseilles, Barcelona, Peñiscola, Valencia, Saragossa, Cuenca, Toledo, Granada, Lisbon, Tarifa, Otranto, Athens, Nicopolis, Constantinople, Smyrna, LESSER ARMENIA, Trebizond, Famagusta, Acre, Alexandria

N S H

Avignon as the Temporary Residence of the Papacy

Avignon was much more central. Stockholm, it was true, was still 1,250 miles off, but Otranto (750 miles), Lisbon (800 miles), Cracow (825 miles) and Edinburgh (900 miles), were all about the same distance away, like the points of a star. But it was not only as the crow flies: for the roads, rivers, and the sea, for the real distances of medieval travel, Avignon was much better situated.

The Rhône valley is the principal break and natural means of communication between the Mediterranean and northern Europe. In the early fourteenth century it connected the two great economic centres of Christendom, that is, central and northern Italy with Flanders: and it connected the great political centres, London and Paris, with Rome and Naples. The Tuscan towns were the principal buyers of English and Burgundian wool and Flemish cloth, and the trade went by sea from Pisa to Provence and Languedoc, up the Rhône–Saône valley (and sometimes that of the Loire) to Paris, the fairs of Champagne, and the English and Flemish towns; and so, back again. By the valleys and passes of the Alps, roads led from the Rhône to Lombardy and the Po valley; from the Rhône, along the valley of the Durance, the coast road led east to Marseilles and Genoa; to the west, land routes led to Spain by the Perthus pass, and on westwards to the Atlantic coast and the Bay of Biscay by the valleys of the Aude and Garonne and through Lodève, Cahors and Perigueux. Lastly, the ports of the lower Rhône from Marseilles to Montpellier dealt with the whole Mediterranean and the Atlantic, with Constantinople, Trebizond, Famagusta, Alexandria, with London and Bruges.

How much this great knot of routes north, south, east and west had made the Rhône valley between Lyons and Arles the true centre of Christendom can be seen from the fact that both the great councils of the later thirteenth century were called at Lyons, in 1245 and 1274; from Clement V's choice of Vienne and then of Lyons for his coronation; and from his calling of the first oecumenical council of the fourteenth century to Vienne in 1311.

The Rhône valley marked the frontier between the Holy

Roman Empire and the kingdom of France; and those towns which bridged the Rhône and could carry road and river traffic were in an admirable position to serve as international meeting-places, and, therefore, international capital cities. Now there were only four bridges over the Rhône in the fourteenth century —at Pont St. Esprit (which is not a town), Lyons, Vienne and Avignon. We have already seen the important part played by Lyons and Vienne in thirteenth- and fourteenth-century Christendom. Avignon had the same advantages as they, but even greater. It was nearer the junction of the Rhône and Durance; consequently, since it was well south of Vienne (90 miles), stopping there did not mean an unnecessary diversion of route for those coming by land from Italy and intending to proceed on to Spain, Aquitaine or Languedoc. Avignon was also nearer the sea. Its bridge was the famous Pont St. Bénézet, the building of which between 1177 and 1185 became the subject of legend, and across it ran the ancient Roman road, the Via Domitia, which had no other way over the Rhône since the ruin of the ancient Roman bridge at Arles. Since that bridge had collapsed the bridge of Avignon was the southernmost to cross the Rhône before it reached the sea. Consequently Avignon reaped the advantages that came from the trade of the estuary. It was the last and most centrally placed of the three great Rhône towns, and it lay like a star in the centre of its roads at the centre of Latin Christendom.

The eighteen-year stay of the papacy revealed all the advantages. John XXII at Avignon had no difficulty in simultaneously negotiating with the kings of France and England, conducting his struggle with Lewis of Bavaria in Germany and Italy, mounting his military expeditions to Lombardy and arming his crusading fleet at Marseilles and Narbonne. Swift messengers took five days to take his letters to Paris or Metz, eight days to Bruges, ten days to London, thirteen to Venice or Rome and, with luck, only thirteen to Naples. Avignon was the point of contact between northern Europe, where the main bulk of Latin Christendom lived, and the Holy Places of Christendom and its ancient centres, Rome and the Holy Land. The Florentine Merchant companies established branches at Avignon from 1317 onwards and made a great commercial centre of it, near the fairs of Beaucaire, St. Gilles and Pézenas. By 1330 it had become the trading and banking centre of Provence and the lower Rhône, substituting itself for Marseilles, ruined by the vain wars in which the French princes of the house of Anjou tried to reconquer Sicily. John XXII found it exceptionally easy to govern Christendom from Avignon, with all parts of which it had such good communications.

III

Avignon as the Normal Residence of the Papacy

There was nothing extraordinary in the fact that the pope was not living in Rome, even if he was living north of the Alps. Again and again since the eleventh century their struggles with the Emperor or the Roman commune had driven the popes from Rome or left them insecure there. They left Rome, and lived, like other contemporary rulers, in a gentle but perpetual itinerary, moving about the Papal States, or even beyond the Alps, where both Innocent IV and Gregory X held their two great councils at Lyons in the thirteenth century. It has been calculated that between 1100 and 1304 the popes spent one hundred and twenty-two years out of Rome as against eighty-two actually in residence.

What was quite unprecedented, however, was that two successive popes, Clement V and John XXII, should never have entered Italy at all. But both wished to go, if only to Bologna, and their wish is evidence of the provisional nature of their stay in Avignon, prolonged though it became.

Things changed when John XXII died. As often happens, the cardinals elected a successor as unlike him as possible. John XXII had transformed ecclesiastical administration and he had despatched military expeditions into Italy: in neither case did the most obvious results seem to justify him—a complete collapse of papal policy in Italy, and a plethora of relations from Quercy established in every administrative office in the papal government, with crying abuses to dishonour the curia. Worse, John was an admirable administrator and clever politician but he had taken his zeal for order and clarity to theology and in

37

his personal capacity as a private theologian had, on All Saints' Day, 1331, preached the doctrine that the souls of all men after death and separation from the body receive the beatific vision of God. The opinion is heterodox, and his enemies, the Fraticelli (or 'Spiritual' Franciscans) and the partisans of Lewis of Bavaria, used this small theological scandal to justify their opposition to him and his deposition by the Emperor—even though it was an *a posteriori* justification, and though the antipope 'Nicholas V' (Peter of Corbara) had already renounced his errors in 1330, and had no successor

The cardinals sought a remedy by electing the most orthodox theologian of the college, Jacques Fournier, a Cistercian monk who took the appropriate name of Benedict XII, for the Cistercians are a branch of the great Benedictine order, then somewhat in decline as a result of the rise of the Friars, but among whom he had made as brilliant a career as a white monk could make.

He had been born of a family in modest circumstances in the county of Foix, and had made his profession as a monk in the Cistercian abbey of Boulbonne from which he had been sent to study theology in the Cistercian College of St. Bernard, in the University of Paris, where he had obtained the doctorate. He was then appointed Abbot of Fontfroide, and shortly afterwards, through the affection of his uncle, the Cistercian cardinal Arnaud Novel, he was, in 1317, created bishop of Pamiers, a diocese in his own home country and one of the surviving refuges of the Albigensian heretics. Assisted by the Inquisition, methodical, meticulous and implacable, learned and austere, he had purified his diocese and reduced the Albigensians to misery and despair, a success which brought him the red hat in 1327; and he had become theologian to the papal court. The election of 1334 was dominated by the need for an orthodox pope and a reformer of administrative abuse. He was learned, he was austere, he was the obvious candidate.

As soon as he became pope he attacked nepotism root and branch. 'The Pope', he is supposed to have said, 'ought to be like Melchisedech—no father, no mother and no genealogy'.

In his constitution *Benedictus Deus* of 1336 he laid down that at death, while the souls of the just enjoy the beatific vision of God, those of the damned are plunged into Hell. He undertook a whole series of reforms to improve the state of the religious orders, above all of the Cistercians who were always close to his heart. But his reforms were too meticulous and detailed to be really effective. It is significant that in this sphere, the one he knew best, he proved to be narrow-minded.

Benedict XII was just as painfully meticulous and careful with the great political and administrative problems with which John XXII had dealt so well. It may be imagined that this studious monk without political experience, devoted above all to peace and poverty, found government, taxation, military organization and diplomacy all alike disconcerting. His honesty and strict virtue were scandalized by the duplicity and treachery of Italian politics. John's armies had met with disaster, the expenses they had created had weighed on every benefice in Christendom, they had corrupted the curia. Benedict saw no reason to continue an Italian policy which was none of his making, and sought to make peace instead. He persuaded King Robert, the French king of 'Sicily' and effective ruler of Naples, to recognize King Frederick of 'Trinacria', the Spaniard who actually ruled Sicily. He made serious concessions to obtain agreements with the lords of the Ghibelline towns, making it his chief condition that they should not support the heretical Lewis of Bavaria. He was forced later to acknowledge that they had deceived him, and that his concessions had involved the loss of all papal influence over Bologna, where he was forced to recognize the disguised lordship of Taddeo Pepoli—the disguise being a nominal tribute—and in the same way all papal influence was lost over Romagna and the Marches. He tried compromise too to bring about Anglo-French agreement over Aquitaine, the French royal succession and Scotland. But he tried in vain to keep the chivalrous Philip VI to his crusading vow in March, 1336 when the situation grew threatening, and his constant efforts could not prevent the outbreak of the Hundred Years War in 1337. Indeed his intransigence may have had something to do with it, in throwing Lewis of Bavaria into the arms of Edward III in March, 1337 by flatly rejecting his overtures for peace with the papacy.

All the same, he had fundamental good sense, and he was never a mere idealist. In many ways his policy continued that of John more than it went against it. He made no weak conciliation with either Lewis of Bavaria or Peter of 'Trinacria', who had no right to occupy Sicily after his father Frederick's death, and he considered that war against these usurpers was a just war. He reinforced the decretals by which his predecessors had nominated to benefices on more and more frequent occasions, but he suppressed abuses and the arbitrary elements in such nominations which were often the source of abuse. Costs and papal taxes on ecclesiastical promotions continued to rise under him, even if he did cut down the expenses of the curia. In this as elsewhere his rigour consisted in making practice conform to principle. His greatest departure stemmed from his realization that he could not go back to Rome: he had been deceived by the Lombards and the lords of the Romagna; civil war raged on in Rome between the Colonna and the Orsini, between people and nobility; so Benedict had to stay on in France and try to reconcile Philip VI and Edward III. He had told his electors he wanted to go back, he had had the roof of St. Peter's repaired; but he could not return, and so, in 1336, he began the reconstruction of the bishop's palace at Avignon, which he turned into a new papal palace.

It may seem astounding that this austere, rigorous, and meticulous pope, more likely than any other, one might think, to desire the return of St. Peter's successor to his mystical bride the Church of Rome, was to undertake the building of a great papal palace in a town which did not even belong to the papacy. There is no need to see Benedict XII as bowing to the will of his cardinals, of whom the majority were from the Langue d'Oc, and for whom the return to Rome would have meant exile. It was an expression of his sound good sense. Once he had realized that there could be no return to Rome and had meditated the obvious advantages of staying in Avignon, he decided to give the papal court the surroundings it needed to function properly. His view of its functions came from canon law, his own tastes, the actual needs of the administration and what the age expected.

He began by abolishing John XXII's expedient to provide the pope with a palace—that the bishopric of Avignon should be left vacant and the diocese be administered by the bishop of Marseilles. He returned to the canon law and in 1336 named a bishop of Avignon, and gave him as palace the residence of a deceased cardinal, also on the Rocher des Doms, but on the other side, the north side of the cathedral. In exchange the bishop made a formal conveyance of his palace to the pope. Benedict XII need now have no scruples in pulling it down and building a new palace for pope and curia.

Round the court of the old bishop's palace, which had no sentimental associations for him, as it had had for John XXII, he built a rather monastic building—cloister, undecorated chapel, high walls. It was also a fortress: Benedict wanted security, and he was afraid of some sudden swoop by Lewis of Bavaria. However, what is less obvious, it was an administrative building as well. The plan may not look like it, but the buildings were designed for the departments they housed, and their size is an expression of what was needed. In building a palace for the pope and curia, with accommodation appropriate to the activities of the Holy See, Benedict XII made it quite clear that he expected to stay at Avignon as long as he was pope. In 1339 he had the papal archives brought from Assisi where they had been since 1304. A great and essential change had taken place: the pope was no longer a guest in a requisitioned house under the protection of an exterior power; he no longer prevented the regular functioning of the Avignon bishopric. He was residing in his own palace, built for him and his administration. It was safe, convenient and adequate. Avignon was no longer the temporary but the normal residence of the popes.

★   ★   ★

Once again, when Benedict died on April 25th, 1342, the cardinals chose a very different type of man, the Cardinal Pierre Roger, who took the name of Clement VI.

Pierre Roger belonged to a family of the lesser nobility of the Limousin. In 1301 he had become a black monk at the great abbey of La Chaise Dieu; his quick intelligence ensured that he was sent to Paris where he gained the doctorate both in theology and canon law. In 1326 he was made abbot of Fécamp in Normandy: already he was renowned for his knowledge and his powers of oratory. In 1328 he was appointed bishop of Arras, in 1329 archbishop of Sens. It was as archbishop of Sens that he had to defend the rights of the ecclesiastical jurisdiction against the royal lawyers at the famous assembly at Vincennes. In 1330 he became archbishop of Rouen, and Philip VI chose him as chancellor of France and he remained as chief minister of the French kingdom till he became cardinal in 1338. Clement VI was a Benedictine monk who had made his career via the episcopate to the red hat, but there any resemblance to Benedict XII ends.

The Limousin is, strictly speaking, in the Langue d'Oc. But it is in northern Aquitaine, though, and Clement had made his career in royal France, in Normandy and Paris. He was the most outstanding French prelate of his time: he had held two archbishoprics and been chancellor and he had full personal experience of the difficult problems which would confront a new pope in this difficult decade. He had spent eight years of his life already trying to solve the worst—the Anglo-French conflict which had culminated in war. He knew peculiarly well the legal problems of the Church, and had seen and known in the Paris Parlement those royal lawyers who represented the rising threats and claims of lay society and the pressures it would bring to bear on the special legal privileges and exemptions of the Church. He was brilliantly intelligent, clear-headed, eloquent and affable; he was brave and showed his courage in the Black Death in 1348; he had wide theological and legal knowledge, political experience, diplomatic skill and charm; he was one of the most talented, able and remarkable men of his time: all this, and a style of life he had learnt at the French court, were what he brought to his task as pope.

Clement VI, like his predecessors, had three major problems, each dependent on the other: the crusade, the Anglo-French conflict, and the Italian lands of the Holy See. Like them he did his best to reconcile the kings of France and England, both of whom he knew and liked so well. He felt particularly deeply Philip VI's defeat at Crécy in 1346 and it was as a result of his indefatigable diplomacy that successive truces were concluded between the two kings.

But unlike Benedict XII who limited his eastern activities to sending help to the Christians of Lesser Armenia, plundered and starved by Turkish invaders, Clement VI did not believe that the divisions of the West should prevent all military action in the East. He realized that the Anglo-French war was likely to be a long one and that waiting for it to end was risking the disappearance of the last Christian states in the East, the kingdom of Lesser Armenia, and the kingdom of Cyprus, which was now the main base of the knights of St. John, the Hospitallers. When he was archbishop of Rouen he had preached the crusade of 1333, which Philip VI was to have led. If no king could lead a crusade, then, like Urban II, Clement saw it as the pope's duty to do so. He prepared an expedition of twenty galleys, of which four were armed at his expense. They sailed to Negropont under the orders of the titular Latin patriarch of Constantinople and had a great victory in capturing Smyrna in October, 1344. On the strength of this, Clement sent another appeal to all the princes of the West, but the only prince to respond was his neighbour Humbert, the Dauphin of Vienne, an uninspiring figure whose crusade went East in 1345 and achieved nothing. When the Christians of the Levant restored Smyrna to the Turks in exchange for a precarious peace and guarantees against piracy, Clement was furious, and refused to sign the treaty. His Eastern policy was that of John XXII, though more energetically pursued. The pope proclaimed himself the leader of Christendom against the infidel, and himself organized the Holy War, realizing that only his success in the

East could re-establish his authority in a Christendom increasingly dominated by powerful national monarchies.

In Italy, despite Benedict XII's recognition of the virtual autonomy of the lords of the cities of the Romagna and the Marches, Clement returned to John's policy, and organized in 1350 a military expedition which he gave to the command of his nephew, Astorge de Durfort, to re-establish the Church's authority in the lost provinces. Astorge, after early success, ran out of money for his mercenaries. The Pepoli handed over Bologna to the Pope's worst enemy, Giovanni Visconti, and Clement could do nothing but save his face by making Visconti the papal vicar of Bologna.

Southern Italy fell into disorder. Joanna I had succeeded her father, King Robert, as queen of French 'Sicily' in 1343: she had married her cousin, Andrew of Hungary, who was murdered in 1345. His brother, King Louis I of Hungary, led an expedition to revenge his brother and seize Naples. Joanna fled to Provence in 1348 where Clement upheld her and supported her. These troubles had repercussions up and down Italy. In Naples in 1342–3 there was a run on the banks after a rumour of the bankruptcy of the big Florentine firms arrived from Flanders and Florence; it was followed by a general crash of the great Florentine banks, the majority of which went bankrupt between 1342 and 1346, seriously damaging the Florentine economy.

This crisis, which affected every commercial centre in the West and the Mediterranean—wherever the Florentine companies had agencies—demonstrates the political and economic solidarity and interdependence of Christendom and, as the crusades showed from another angle, the way in which events in one part of Christendom immediately affected the rest. There was an economic, military and political crisis in the West in these years, which the Black Death of 1348–51 turned into a physical and moral catastrophe with the sudden death of about a third of the population of Christendom.

The effects of the plague and of the whole interconnected crisis struck Florence and Naples particularly and helped the

44

decline of the Guelf alliance. It might, therefore, have given occasion for a Ghibelline revival and for a renewal of the imperial interest in Italy. But Lewis of Bavaria was old and disregarded and the German Electors had deposed him in 1346, while the new 'King of the Romans' they had elected was Charles of Moravia, whom Clement VI had known at the French court and who had neither any immediate desire to be crowned Emperor in Rome nor any Italian ambitions.

Rome was not likely to avoid the ruins, wars, or disasters of Italy. Still the Colonna and the Orsini fought on; and still the popular party fought the nobility. In 1343 the popular party found a remarkable leader in a mystically-minded lawyer, Cola di Rienzo. Rienzo's head was full of old texts from Roman historians and old inscriptions which still could be read in the city, and which at this period were now receiving new attention, research and copyists. He was encouraged by Petrarch in an idea of Renaissance—the Renaissance of the Roman people to regovern Rome, Italy and the Empire. It was to be a Christian Rome, however, an Empire which included Christendom and the papacy which had given Rome a new kind of rule over Europe. Rienzo used the sign of the Holy Ghost and he demanded that the pope should return to the City, which, as he said on the coins he struck, was mistress of the world. At an antiquarian, almost archeological ceremony on the Capitol he took the title of 'Rector' of Rome, a title which it would be extremely difficult for the pope to accept; and then in May, 1347, he proclaimed himself 'Tribune'—'Nicholas, By the Will of JESUS CHRIST, knight of the Holy Ghost, severe and merciful liberator of Rome and zealot of Italy, great friend of the World, Tribune, Augustus'. This set of titles could only mean that he was usurping papal rights over the City and the Empire.

Yet once again the state of Italy, violent, variously and chronically disordered, plainly prevented any return by Clement VI to Rome. He had realized the situation clearly when he became pope and it may safely be said that he never thought of such a return. He said so plainly and without any beating about the bush to the Roman embassy (which included

45

Cola di Rienzo) when they came to congratulate him on his election in 1343 and to announce to him that the Romans had chosen him personally and for life as Syndic, Rector, Captain and Defender of the Roman people. He would not, he said, go back because the Anglo-French war claimed all his attention and because Rome was much too disturbed. As a consolation he did proclaim the year 1350 as a Jubilee and the mass of pilgrims who came to Rome that year did bring money with them.

Thus, from his election on, Clement VI settled at Avignon with no thought of leaving it. He had come from the luxurious and chivalrous court of France and he intended that his own court should be worthy of the first sovereign in the world: that it should be the most splendid and the most ceremonious. He multiplied court offices and filled many of them with his relations and friends from the Limousin, his widehanded generosity attracted great flocks of the clergy looking for papal provisions to benefices, he increased the administration and he organized ceremonies and festivals for the great Christian feasts and for the arrivals and departures of kings and princes. In short, he wanted to make the papal court the social centre of Christendom.

All this activity and brilliance took more room than there was in Benedict XII's palace. Clement VI, therefore, started to build a second palace next to his predecessor's, but, as might be expected, grander and more magnificent. Common sense and custom alike dictated that from the outside it should still look like a fortress. Inside, though, there was nothing austere or monastic about Clement's palace: the enormous rooms were decorated with frescoes, the audience room, above all the great chapel, were worthy of a sovereign pontiff. The chapel was on the first floor, and on the landing outside it a huge bay window was built with magnificent tracery through which the pope could bless the crowd below. Clement's court had style and grandeur. 'My predecessors', he said, 'did not know how to be popes'. Indeed, Clement, enterprising, generous, magnificent, *was* the greatest monarch of his day. Profiting from the difficulties of Queen Joanna he bought the town of Avignon from her in 1348 for 80,000 florins and the new 'King of the Romans', Charles of Moravia, renounced all imperial sovereignty over the town. The pope was now ruler of Avignon as well as of the Comtat Venaissin. He established his Mint in the city.

The building of the second palace and the buying of Avignon marked Clement's decision to live permanently on the Rhône. Petrarch was furiously annoyed, but in vain: there the pope was, in a really papal palace, no longer any other ruler's guest, or in any relationship which risked dependence, with sufficient power, a strongly-fortified residence and a splendid court, all to make him at home and secure, and as sovereign over the town where he was living as he would be in Bologna or Rome. Avignon was now a capital city, one of the great capitals of the world. In the last years of Clement VI it was at its zenith. Clement's temperament, ideas and means were very different from those of his predecessors, but he followed their policy (which had in some ways progressed and developed without their knowing it) and it had led him to his achievement.

However, in the very moment when Clement had firmly installed himself in papal majesty at Avignon he proclaimed the Jubilee of 1350 which drew Christians in crowds to Rome. Such a pilgrimage could only be made to the tombs of the apostles Peter and Paul. The Black Death of 1348–50 ensured that the pilgrimage would be a success—and many who had been spared went on it in thanksgiving. Some of them passed through Avignon, but it was to Rome that they were going. The Jubilee coincided with Avignon's pinnacle of power and prestige, and the contrast was the problem that seemed pressing and glaring to many people, especially in Italy. The Pope lived at Avignon where he was now happily settled, well-equipped to perform his office as Head of Christendom and chief administrator of the Church. But Rome was where St. Peter and St. Paul had died; Rome was the city of which the pope was bishop as St. Peter's successor; Rome was the spiritual capital of Christendom. Rome or Avignon? Good Christians were distressed that there even seemed to be a choice. Nor, in fact, was there: the pope could not return to the Italian states of the Church in the state they were in. The papal legate, Annibaldo di Ceccano, narrowly escaped death at the hands of two assassins while making his personal pilgrimage to the four great basilicas of Rome during the Jubilee—that alone showed how right Clement was not to think of return. If he ever were to re-establish his temporal authority in Italy, though, it would be difficult for him to resist the call of Rome. St. Bridget of Sweden came to Rome for the Jubilee in 1350 and lived there awaiting the Pope's return, and she symbolizes the mystical hope of those anxious souls who awaited the return of the Shepherd to the flock of Peter.

★   ★   ★

Clement VI's policies of prestige and action were undoubtedly successful: in the monarchical, aristocratic terms of the century they underlined that the successor of St. Peter was the leader of the world; they increased the pope's control over the clergy at large. But they were expensive. The acquisition of Avignon, the building of the second palace, the two crusades, the festivities and luxury of the papal court, all gradually emptied the Treasury filled by Benedict XII's austere parsimony. It will be remembered that Clement VI was forced to leave his nephew Astorge de Durfort in the financial lurch when he was campaigning in the Romagna in 1350. Prestige was useful, but it was so expensive that it involved the sacrifice of papal power in the states of the Church—one of the essential aims of papal policy.

Consequently, when Clement died on December 6th, 1352, the conclave looked for a successor who would be less extravagant and flamboyant, and would remedy the dangers which the cardinals saw as inherent in Clement's policy. They were disquieted by the tendency on the part of the late pope to a purely personal government, made possible by his intelligence, eloquence, generosity, activity and popularity. They therefore drew up, and nearly all signed, as a preliminary to the conclave, an agreement that the Sacred College as a body should be superior to the pope. They then elected an elderly man in poor health, the Grand Penitentiary Etienne Aubert, whom they thought unlikely to pursue grandiose policies or to make things difficult for themselves—who would be harmless. He took the name Innocent VI.

As far as background went, there was no change from recent tradition: Etienne Aubert was another Frenchman from the Langue d'Oc, another native of the Limousin like Clement VI, a lawyer who had taught canon law at the university of Toulouse, a friend of the King of France, for whom he had acted as judge in the seneschalcy of Toulouse and whom he had known in the four years when he had been bishop of Noyon in northern France and Clermont in Auvergne before he had been made a cardinal in 1342.

Innocent VI had only signed the agreement conditionally, and he had the wisdom to annul it as uncanonical. But if he had had any intention of following in Clement's footsteps he did not have the means. The palace was finished. The Anglo-French war got worse as it continued; France was in a desperate state of peasant revolt and political collapse after the defeat and capture of King John the Good by the Black Prince at Poitiers in 1356. No further crusade could conceivably be attempted. Clement VI's successes had been fleeting for all his energy, and that underlined the fact (which by now hardly needed underlining) that there could be no lasting success against the Saracens without the union of France and England.

Weighing up the situation, Innocent VI concluded that the first necessity for the Church was order in the Papal States, and on that he concentrated all the resources he could muster. He was lucky enough to find the perfect man for the task in the college of cardinals, a man whose exceptional talents had been realized by Clement VI, whose abilities were very similar—Cardinal Albornoz.

Gil Alvarez Carillo Albornoz was a member of a noble family in Cuença, and, like Innocent VI himself, had studied canon law at Toulouse. He became Primate of Spain and archbishop of Toledo in 1338 and was a principal figure in the

D 49

reign of Alfonso XI of Castile, playing an important part in the Reconquista of Spain—it was his personal action which decided the victory of Tarifa in the crusade of 1340. In 1348 it was he who drew up the Constitutions of Alcala to reconcile the vast number of clashing municipal customs and to restore peace to the kingdom. He was a knight and a statesman, with a peculiarly Castilian pride which led him to leave Toledo for the curia with dignity in 1350 when a quarrel rose between him and the new king of Castile, Pedro II, the cruel, in which he felt his honour to be at stake.

No better pacificator and organizer could have been found for the task than this experienced warrior and grand seigneur, and Innocent VI named him legate for all Italy and Vicar-General in all the states of the Church on June 30th, 1353, and charged him to re-establish the authority of the Holy See.

Albornoz did not begin in the north, as geography and John XXII did. He started in the south, from Rome, where the recent Jubilee had revived a desire for the pope's return. In the north, for the time being, without greater authority, prestige, and outside help, he had no hope of prevailing against the Visconti. He took oaths of fealty from loyal barons, raised a militia from loyal towns and proceeded to hire mercenaries.

He was strikingly successful. He drove Giovanni di Vico by main force out of Viterbo and Orvieto. He had the wisdom to make a treaty with Giovanni which left him some of his possessions and enabled him to put himself and them under the protection of the pope. Albornoz then (1354–5) called a Parliament of all the pope's vassals at Montefiascone, the capital of the Patrimony of St. Peter. He summoned as well representatives from all the Communes of the Patrimony to swear to observe his Constitutions for the Patrimony. The Constitutions left vassals and communes alike their property, liberty and privileges, but placed them fairly and squarely under the sovereignty of the pope (1354–5). Albornoz was at once soldier, peacemaker and lawyer, and it was the combination of gifts, all of them necessary, which enabled him to reconquer the Duchy of Spoleto (1355), the March of Ancona (1355) and the Romagna (1356–7).

The Constitutions which he published in the Parliament of Fano in 1357 for the March of Ancona will serve as a model for his policy, based on years of experience and careful thought: it was to give the States of the Church a common basis by means of unification and codification of their laws, unification of their administration, but to allow for the continuing existence of various separate classes of city each with their own statutes and customs—all this to accompany the firm reinforcement of all the various ties of allegiance which bound the cities and provinces of the papal lands to the Holy See. The States of the Church were much more the pope's lands than his *State*, but Albornoz in effect founded the Papal State by unifying law, abolishing multiplicity of custom, bad and antiquated custom which led to privileges and exceptions. The constitutions of Fano acted as the prototype for other provincial constitutions and the whole collection of constitutions formed the so-called 'Aegidian' Constitutions—named after Gil (Latin 'Aegidius') Albornoz—which regulated the laws and life of the Papal State until 1816.

As he had foreseen, Albornoz's task was hardest in the Romagna, the last province he had left to tackle, where he knew that his chief enemy would be Bernabò Visconti, who did not intend under any circumstances to abandon control of Bologna or his client tyrants in the Romagnol cities. Visconti knew his danger, and set diplomacy and gold to work at Avignon to get Albornoz recalled. He was successful, and the Spanish cardinal was replaced by the incompetent abbot of Cluny, Androin de la Roche, for one year, 1357–8. But Innocent VI soon saw his mistake, and renewed the legation for Albornoz. Albornoz again had a series of striking successes and on October 27th, 1360, made his solemn entry into Bologna: the new Emperor, Charles IV, by joining him against Bernabò in 1361, prevented any successful counter-attack.

Charles IV's help was as precious to Albornoz as Lewis of Bavaria's hostility had been damaging to Bertrand du Poujet in the time of John XXII. Charles IV was on excellent terms with the pope. He might have German wars and ambitions— but he had no desire to meddle in the quarrels of Italy where his predecessors had wasted so much energy. Although he wanted to be crowned Emperor to benefit from the authority and prestige of the imperial title, he did not intend to make his journey to Rome an occasion for Ghibelline demonstrations or recovery, or wish to prevent the re-establishment of papal power. He fell in with all Innocent VI's demands and wishes. He came to Rome rapidly, almost incognito, with a small escort. The only day he was *officially* in Rome was Easter Sunday, 1355, when he was crowned by the legate in St. Peter's. He left on Easter Monday. There had never before been an imperial coronation which had not plunged Italy in war, or which had not meant much bloodshed at Rome. Charles IV might treat papal authority over the Empire cavalierly in Germany, but in Italy his attitude was an enormous assistance to Albornoz's re-conquest: a friendly Emperor who would raise no difficulties made it much easier for the pope to go home.

Not that Innocent VI thought of Rome as home, any more than his predecessors, and naturally enough, for war raged on in Italy up till his death in 1362. In France the Anglo-French war only stopped in 1360, with the Treaty of Calais, disastrous for France, and with preliminaries of the Treaty of Brétigny. King John had only just been ransomed from captivity. The various cessions of territory specified in the Treaty had yet to take place and its clauses had yet to be put into effect. Papal diplomacy was still working desperately for peace. John the Good announced that he would visit Innocent in 1362 to discuss it all; but Innocent died on September 12th, 1362, just before the royal visit. Even given peace in Italy, he could not have left Avignon.

Innocent had had difficulties which his predecessors had not had to face. The successive truces in the Anglo-French war from 1356 onwards, and the final peace in 1360 loosed upon France the unemployed and unpaid mercenaries. The papal court was full of fabulous treasures, crowded with rich prelates, fat businessmen and Italian bankers with full coffers. It made a tempting prey. One mercenary, Arnauld de Cervole, made a raid in 1357. Another settled down at Pont St. Esprit in 1360

with his company and besieged Avignon. The town was reduced to starvation and had to pay ransom to get rid of him.
The two attacks alarmed both townsmen and curia. In 1357
the Pope—whose business as the town's ruler it now was—had
to take defensive measures. In 1360 he started to wall the town
with a battlemented wall and fortified gates. It was another
step in the relationship between the pope and Avignon. The
pope was now sovereign, the town was his, he must protect it
as well as his own palace. Avignon now lived on the pope and
by his protection.

★   ★   ★

The conclave which followed Innocent's death was divided
into two readily recognizable factions: Limousin and non-
Limousin. The Limousin cardinals were the creations of the
last two popes, and they were roughly equal in numbers to the
others. In the end the cardinals took the solution of the conclave of Perugia and looked outside the college. They chose—
easily—Guillaume de Grimoard, abbot of St. Victor's, Marseilles, who took the name Urban V on October 31st, 1362.

Guillaume de Grimoard was born in 1310 at Grisac of a
noble family in the Gévaudan. He became a monk at the
priory of Chirac and then went successively to the universities
of Montpellier, Toulouse, Avignon and Paris, and taught canon
law. He was abbot in turn of the great Benedictine abbeys
of St. Germanus at Auxerre (1352–61) and St. Victor at Marseilles (1361–2). Like all his recent predecessors he came from
the Langue d'Oc, though this time from the Massif Central and
he had always lived or studied in the Rhône valley. Like them
he was a scholar and a canon lawyer, like Benedict XII and
Clement VI he belonged to the great family of monks and he
had directed very important abbeys. He had many of Benedict's and Clement's characteristics, but there was also a considerable difference: he had never been a bishop or a cardinal,
he had been scarcely touched by Church administration or
papal diplomacy, and he had never served the king of France
or had anything to do with his court.

53

GENERAL MAP SHOWING TOWNS, PROVINCES AND STATES
MENTIONED IN THE TEXT

Avignon as the Normal Residence of the Papacy

The career he had had, removed from the major problems
of administration and contemporary politics, explains part of
the new pope's character: Urban was above all a man preoccupied with developing learning, with increasing the knowledge and religion of students or monks who came under his
direction, so that they might be orthodox in their belief and add
spiritual depth to their lives. He was a genuinely religious man,
and a very good one, and his austerity and simplicity had
already given him a reputation for sanctity. He was a true
monk, at once learned and holy: it was because he continued
to practise these virtues as pope that he is the only one of the
Avignon popes that the Church has canonized. The cardinals
elected him because, since Marseilles is near Avignon, they
knew him and admired his learning and sanctity and because
Innocent VI had sent him on a number of missions to Sicily,
which gave him some experience of Italian questions. Urban V
was then eminent intellectually and morally, totally independent
of the factions which rent the sacred college, and objective with
regard to the problems which faced him.

His goodness and his desire to spread learning were shown in
his generosity to a large number of churches and communities
in the Gévaudan, to the cathedral of Mende, to a number of
Benedictine abbeys, including Monte Cassino, and the principal
universities: he loved founding colleges for poor students, the
most important of his foundations being the college of St.
Benedict and St. Germanus at Montpellier—St. Benedict and
St. Germanus were the two saints he most reverenced.

Urban V was a good man and an objective one and both
these qualities made him take a new look at the problems which
previous popes straight from the cardinalate had viewed with
experienced, but biassed and weary eyes. Urban was a methodical canon lawyer and he continued his predecessors' policy of
centralization and he continued too to furnish and improve the
papal palace, to which, like a good Benedictine, he added a
garden for peace, recollection and tranquillity: he continued
also to wall the town of Avignon, giving the job to his brother,
Anglic Grimoard, whom he had made a bishop. But he had

55

no preconceived notions on what seemed to him the most important problems—the crusade, and where the pope should live.

Innocent VI had not had leisure for the East. Turkish pressure on the Christian kingdoms and the Byzantine Empire was becoming harder and harder. The Turks had taken Gallipoli in 1356 and settled in Europe. The new king of Cyprus, Peter I of Lusignan, had counter-attacked and had great success in Cilicia with the capture of Attalia and Myra in 1360; he had then come west to look for help and made a long recruiting voyage from 1362 on, beating-up enthusiasm for a crusade which his own successes made seem likely, for once, to be successful. John the Good, king of France, that mirror of chivalry, took the cross although barely out of an English prison, and discussed the problem with Urban just after Urban became pope. Urban was naturally interested, even if this crusade, so far, owed nothing to any activities of his own. There was at last peace between England and France—not likely, it is true, to be either complete or lasting, but it made Urban hopeful. It seemed to him right and proper to direct all Christian military effort eastwards, and with that end in view Urban set an example by ending the war between the Church and Bernabò Visconti, already beaten by Albornoz. Thus all the companies of mercenaries would be unemployed in both France and Italy and could leave for the East to beat the Turk, help the Byzantine Empire, bring about the reunion of Christendom, and deliver the Holy Places. In 1364 Urban V made Albornoz sign an unexpectedly favourable and unhoped-for peace with Milan: Bernabò Visconti was to retain the juridical title of Vicar of the Church at Bologna until, over the next eight years, he had been paid an indemnity of 500,000 florins.

Urban's policy was naïve despite its high motives. Men did not think as he did in the second half of the fourteenth century. If John the Good did, he was a man of the previous generation in his thinking, and he died in England where he had honourably returned to prison till his ransom was paid. His son, Charles V, had not the slightest intention of going East: all his efforts were bent on not fulfilling his obligations under the treaty of Brétigny.

Bernabò Visconti equally had no intention whatsoever of using the Church's indemnity for the purpose for which it was given—raising a crusading army. As for the mercenaries, they would far rather ravage a defenceless Christendom than face as tough an adversary as the Turk. Urban was a holy and openly straightforward man, but he could get no one to promise definitely to assist the king of Cyprus, or attack the Saracen, or help the Greek Emperor at a moment of crisis so serious that the Byzantines were once more thinking of union.

This failure shows very well how weak papal authority had become. Urban V had taken the name of Urban II (who had preached the first crusade); however, moved as he had been by the highest motives, his preaching found no echo or answer among the princes or peoples of the West.

It was with the same high principles that Urban viewed the problem of where the pope was to live. There is no doubt that he liked Avignon: he had improved the palace and it was near his home and the whole surroundings of his previous life. But St. Peter and his successors were bishops of *Rome*: the papal court was the curia *Romana*; papal bulls were sealed with heads of the apostles Peter and Paul. Urban was strict and had received a monastic training. He was attacking absenteeism and trying to make bishops reside in their dioceses, he could not himself set such a bad example. Though Petrarch might be extravagant and bombastic, there was truth in the picture he painted of Rome widowed by her spiritual husband and true protector. Moreover, events in the East did make reunion seem more likely. Conversations ought to be opened with the Byzantine Emperor John V Palaeologus. Rome was the best place for them: the dissension lay between New Rome and Old Rome; the schism lay between the pope of Rome and the patriarch of Constantinople, and it was with a pope *at* Rome that the Greeks ought to deal. Apart from this feeling of propriety, the geographical position of Rome was much better once the East was important again: it might be on one edge of Latin Christendom, but it was central to a reunited Christendom which would stretch to the Bosphorus and the Dnieper.

All this made Urban want to return. The major difficulties which had prevented his predecessors from doing so had disappeared. For the first time since 1337 peace had been concluded between England and France: it might be precarious but Urban was not going to look gift horses in the mouth. Albornoz had reconquered and reorganized the states of the Church and all his work and all the costly Italian policy of the popes since John XXII would be vain and pointless if it did not mean the pope's return to Rome now it had come to success. So said Albornoz. Finally, Rome itself was calmer. A new popular constitution had been established in 1360, supported and defended by a popular militia, the *Felix Societas Balestriorum et Pavesatorum*, whose leaders formed part of the government of the commune. They had expelled the nobles, achieved order in the city and scared away from it the mercenary companies who were now insulting and endangering Avignon.

Urban had not lived at Avignon before he was pope. He was a religious and plain-thinking man, more open than his predecessors and less easily argued round. His presence at Avignon since the peace was less necessary to the king of France, whom, again unlike his predecessors, he had never served. Under all the circumstances Urban decided in 1365 to re-establish the Holy See in Rome. The movement of such a great court with its hangers-on, its archives, its supplies, posed hitherto unknown problems of transport and of continuity in government. It seems likely that it was the sheer difficulty and expense of moving quite as much as the fact that many of the cardinals and curia came from Provence or Languedoc that had made the curia hesitant about leaving. Was it practicable to move? After numerous careful preparations Urban V, preceded by furniture and supplies and accompanied by a deputation of cardinals and the main body of the curia, left Avignon on April 30th, 1367, and on May 19th embarked at Marseilles for Rome.

IV

The Papacy Returns to Avignon, 1367–1403

The fleet which carried the pope and the curia arrived at Corneto, the chief port of the Patrimony, on June 3rd, 1367. Urban V was welcomed by Albornoz who presented him, so to speak, as he stepped ashore, with the states of the Church which he had won back. After spending the summer at Viterbo, the largest town of the Patrimony, the pope entered Rome on October 16th. The Lateran palace was uninhabitable and Urban therefore took up residence at the Vatican where the popes have lived ever since.

The curia had not entirely left Avignon with him. A great administrative machine of the fourteenth century could not move about its departments and archives in the manner of the constantly travelling kings and popes of the thirteenth century without gravely impairing its efficiency. It was even more impossible for the greatest of administrations, which extended its activities to the whole Christian world, especially when the move involved a sea journey and fifteen days away from any major centre. The government of the Church could not afford a fifteen-day vacuum. Urban V and his chamberlain, Arnaud Aubert, therefore, did not organize a two-stage move, but quite simply duplicated departments so that continuity should be maintained.

Urban V took with him the college of cardinals, the papal Chamberlain and his department the 'Camera Apostolica' or Papal Chamber, the Chancery, the Penitentiary, the curialists themselves and a large quantity of furniture, baggage and provisions. But a small part of the administration and much the greater part of the accumulation which had resulted from sixty years' continuous residence in the palace at Avignon was left in the charge of Philip of Cabassole, Patriarch of Jerusalem, whom Urban had appointed Governor of Avignon, Vicar General of the bishopric, Rector of the Comtat Venaissin and Warden of the palace. The large majority of the employees of the Camera stayed behind with the second-in-command, the papal Treasurer, to look after them; with him were two of the four clerks of the Camera. The papal Treasury stayed with them, part of it in the Treasure Tower of the palace, and papal finance continued to be administered at Avignon. Many clerks and notaries of the Chancery also stayed at Avignon, and Urban V left his library there as well.

While the curia was en route to Rome the members of the Camera who had been left at Avignon continued to manage the financial life of the Church and this state of things continued after the Chamberlain had established himself at the Vatican. Avignon was so well situated for dealing with northern countries: it had become a very important commercial centre and it was so customary to send cash there and make transfers via Avignon that during the years 1367–70 the Camera at Avignon continued to take in money and pay it out and was even in the position of subsidising the Camera at Rome.

The papal court, in fact, had not really left Avignon for Rome. It had been cut in two, the most important half being with the pope and cardinals at Rome, but the other half at Avignon while less important was still very active. There were two administrative centres: administratively and financially Avignon dealt with northern Christendom as intermediary for the curia at Rome.

At Rome Urban V did what could only be done at St. Peter's, above all at St. Peter's tomb: he solemnly received Charles IV for instance, in 1368; but above all, on October 18th, 1369, he received the Emperor of Constantinople, John V Palaeologus who, in return for renouncing the schism and making a public submission to the pope, hoped for Western help against the Turkish threat to Byzantium. Urban V's dreams of a crusade and union of the churches seemed very near fruition.

The Papacy Returns to Avignon, 1367–1403

It was just at this moment that the smouldering French war, damped down inefficiently by the treaty of Brétigny-Calais, burst into flame. Charles V had reorganized his kingdom and was profiting from the weakness of the ageing Edward III to undo the consequences of his father's defeat. Charles had decided to hear the appeal made to his court by the count of Armagnac against the Black Prince as duke of Aquitaine. That was in 1368, and on November 30th, 1369, Charles V solemnly pronounced the consequent forfeiture of Aquitaine, as Philip VI had done in 1337. War began once more and in 1369 and 1370 two mounted English expeditions ravaged France.

These events in the West shattered Urban's hopes in the East. To try to re-establish peace between England and France, upon which, as Urban thought, there depended the good of the Christian East and the union of the churches, Urban V decided to return to Avignon, where it was easier to negotiate with Charles and Edward. Perhaps Albornoz might have kept him in Italy; but Albornoz had died in 1367. Without telling the Romans of his intention Urban left Rome to spend the summer at Viterbo and Montefiascone and from thence, despite the prophetic warnings of St. Bridget of Sweden, took ship from Corneto for Marseilles on September 4th, 1370. He and the curia entered Avignon on September 4th, 1370, but shortly afterwards Urban fell sick, and on December 19th he died.

Avignon was once more the home of the papacy and the sole capital of Christendom, for Urban had left no administration in Rome.

★   ★   ★

On January 5th, 1371, the conclave elected the Cardinal Pierre Roger de Beaufort, who took the name Gregory XI.

Gregory XI was from Limousin and nephew to Clement VI, who had made him a cardinal when he was nineteen years old in 1348, and he may well have seemed to incarnate all the nepotism of the popes from the Langue d'Oc who had succeeded one another since Clement V's time. But the early age at which he had received the red hat made the Cardinal de

Beaufort different from all his predecessors. He had never been either abbot or bishop, he had never served a king; on the other hand, he knew Italy very well and had lived there for some time. As soon as he was made cardinal in 1348 he had gone to Perugia to sit under Piero Baldi degli Ubaldi, one of the most famous legal scholars then living. Like so many cardinals Gregory was a lawyer—though a civil lawyer as well as a canon lawyer. In Perugia and Tuscany he had made the acquaintance of a certain number of humanists; he was interested in literature and the arts. His health was poor and this helped to make him studious and bookish. Clement VI, his uncle, was a Maecenas, but Gregory XI was the first humanist pope. That does not mean, however, that he was not pious: he was deeply religious and had a strong bent and feeling for things spiritual. Italian politics had developed his knowledge of the world, had made him realistic and a great diplomat. By sheer seniority he came to hold a certain authority among the cardinals and while Urban V was in Rome between 1367 and 1370 he had been one of the most prominent cardinals and the pope had frequently entrusted him with responsibility in the city. His Roman experience complemented the knowledge he had gained in Perugia. He knew the new humanism in all its first fervour. He was, therefore, one of the cardinals best qualified to solve the papacy's problems in Rome and Italy.

In fact his opinion was both formed and firm. The first duty of the papacy was the crusade—to frustrate the infidel and reunite the churches—and the name he took, Gregory XI, harked back to Blessed Gregory X, the pope of the thirteenth century whose whole policy had been turned to crusading. The Emperor John's visit in 1369 and his renunciation of the schism had made it plain that Rome was the right place for active and efficient eastern relations. Besides Gregory had personally observed the disquiet occasioned among the powers in Italy by Albornoz's reconquest of the papal states, which they had hoped to absorb. The pope's residence in Rome made the Papal State a power in politics, and his absence only sharpened the appetite of its neighbours. As soon as Gregory came to the papal throne he was forced to undertake a series of wars—first, in 1371, against Perugia to reduce it to obedience and second, from 1371 to 1375, against the Visconti who still pursued their aim of building up Milanese power in the Romagna and Piedmont. He was forced to cope with the bitterness of the Florentines whose hope of ruling all Tuscany, papal and non-papal alike, was stronger than their traditional 'Guelfism' which, if it means anything at all means 'Papalism'. All this reinforced Gregory's belief that the only way to retain the Papal State was to govern it from Rome. Lastly, his Roman contacts both with the commune and with all levels of Roman society made him sensitive to the real possibility that the Romans, left without a bishop, might well look for another pope, another antipope, like Peter of Corbara, and start a schism—even if this time it would not have an emperor to back it.

Contrary to everything one might have expected of his uncle's nephew, Gregory XI's piety, policy and past all determined his decision to take the Holy See back to Rome. He said so quite plainly and frequently. But a whole series of unfavourable circumstances forced him to postpone the journey.

Firstly, the treasury was empty. Since the great era of building at Avignon and Cardinal Albornoz's wars the careful accumulations of Benedict XII had all vanished. Since Urban V an overdraft had come to stay and the treasury lived on borrowed money. This alone discouraged an expensive move—which had been made once and once was enough to show just how enormous the expense was.

A large number of cardinals and a clear majority of the curia were at pains to underline any difficulties they could find. They were natives of Southern France and did not want to leave home. They could no longer say that Rome was insecure, and the argument was not even raised when Urban went to Rome; but they said that it was plain from Urban's stay there that it was impracticable for the pope to live in Rome. If he left Avignon he would have to come back because Western affairs were so much more important and were, eventually, the determinants of any crusade. The king of France repeated himself, and got others to repeat for him: 'Rome is wherever the pope happens to be'.

The course of the Anglo-French war (which peculiarly affected Gregory XI's native Limousin) reinforced such arguments.

Gregory XI sent legate after legate to Charles V and Edward III to bring about negotiations and truce. However, the consequent conferences at Calais in 1372 and Bruges in 1373 did nothing to halt hostilities. The new conference at Bruges in 1374 seemed more hopeful and Gregory put off his return to Rome for a year. In spring, 1375, his nuncios did obtain a truce for a year and once more the pope put off his return to try to preserve the truce and to turn it into peace. As for the East, an attempt at organizing a crusade came to nothing in 1372, and in 1373 the Byzantine Emperor, John V Palaeologus, signed a peace treaty with the Sultan Murad, knowing that he could expect no help. At the same time the Egyptians overran Lesser Armenia. Everything made it plain that nothing save a great and concerted effort from the kings of the West could do anything there.

At this moment the Florentines, more and more disquieted by the reorganization of the Papal State, found in this delay a pretext for discrediting Gregory with Italian opinion. They seized the occasion of the refusal of export licences of grain from the Papal State into Tuscany, because of the famine of 1375, by the French papal administrators, to construct a league of all the neighbouring powers who had territorial ambitions in the Papal State against the pope's Vicars—and therefore against the pope. This was the end of the traditional 'Guelf' alliance. Florence was both too powerful and too ambitious to tolerate a strong Papal State at her doors. Rather than that, she was prepared to attack her oldest ally, even at the cost of losing her bankers their biggest customer. Derisively, Florence nicknamed the eight magistrates who directed the war the 'Eight Saints'— from which the 'War of the Eight Saints' gets its name. In a few months Bologna and other principal towns had revolted and the Papal State seemed lost to the Church.

Gregory used all his diplomacy and kept his head. He laid an interdict on Florence, her allies and the rebellious towns, he hired the footloose companies of Breton and Gascon mercenaries left free by the truce between France and England, and he directed them, under the generalship of the Cardinal Robert of Geneva, against the states of the Church which they reconquered without much difficulty. At length, too, against all advice, Gregory decided to move the papacy irrevocably to Rome in 1376 so that he could rule the reconquered provinces himself and take up the fight with Florence. It is possible that his poor health had made him hesitate to take a step which he had clearly and finally decided upon for years, and that he saw the hand of God in the arrival of St. Catherine of Siena at Avignon to urge his return. There has been a pointless scholarly controversy on this issue. Who knows the secrets of hearts?

It was on September 13th, 1376, that Gregory XI and the curia left Avignon for Marseilles. Urban V's return had taught useful lessons which, nine years later, were still remembered. Papal administration must go on functioning during the journey. That the journey was made in autumn meant that Gregory would certainly be in Rome all winter, and the diplomatic situation required a whole series of complex negotiations with Italian princes and towns which were likely to keep him there. Gregory therefore left a rather more important and numerous set of officials at Avignon than Urban V had done. An innovation was that a committee of cardinals was left responsible for negotiations with the French and English kings, for the ambassadors at Bruges, and for the government and protection of Avignon and the Comtat Venaissin. As in 1367, the papal Treasurer and the Clerk of the Camera were left behind, as was the Vice-Chancellor with various departments of the Chancery. The archives and the papal library were not moved and copies —not the originals—of the papal registers were to be sent to Rome. Thus a well-staffed section of the administration stayed at Avignon and looked after the Church in the following five months. Still, it was only a section, and the burden was crushing. As in 1367–70, for the whole of 1377 the northern revenues of the Church were banked at Avignon and Avignon financed the Camera in Rome by sea.

The majority of the curia, however, were en route for Rome. The general opinion of the move seems well summed-up by Pierre Ameilh, bishop of Senigallia (who wrote a description of the papal journey in Leonine verse), when he describes the pass near Orgon where the road runs between the mountains and the river Durance. 'God!', he says, 'If only the mountains would move and stop our journey!' Just the same, the pope took ship on October 3rd. A long coastal journey followed, made necessary by the negotiations with Genoa, Pisa, Lucca, Florence and Siena. The ships were storm-tossed by winter winds, which seemed to breathe ill omens and misfortune; at length the fleet anchored at Corneto on December 5th and then entered the mouth of the Tiber and sailed up to Rome, which the pope solemnly entered on January 13th, 1377.

Florence signed peace that year after a series of conferences at Sarzana, arranged by the Visconti. Gregory XI had saved the Papal State by returning to Rome, but the breakdown of the conference at Bruges and the Wycliffite troubles in England were part of the price he paid—Anglo-French war, English particularism, and criticism by the English clergy of the Church's whole structure and administration. There can be no doubt at all either that Gregory's early death from exhaustion and weariness was a major tragedy for the whole Church. He died at the Vatican on March 27th, 1378.

★   ★   ★

After the funeral the conclave met on April 7th, 1378, at the Vatican. There were sixteen cardinals in Rome and they were acutely divided. Roughly speaking there were three groups—the men from the Limousin, the other French and the Italians. This division was one difficulty. The other was the attitude of the Roman people.

For the Romans this was the first conclave since 1303 and immensely important. The return of pope and curia had been very welcome: it had restored the city's normal religious life, it

Ferrara

Bologna

ROMAGNA

Cesena

Rimini

Florence

Fano

Senigallia

Ancona

Arno

MARCH

OF

ANCONA

Siena

Lake
Trasimene

TUSCANY

DUCHY

Ascoli

Perugia

Assisi

OF

Cascia

Orvieto

SPOLETO

Lake of
Bolsena

Montefiascone

Viterbo

*Sabine
Hills*

PATRIMONY

OF

ST. PETER

Corneto

Tiber

Rieti

Sulmona

Civitavecchia

Lake
Bracciano

KINGDOM

OF

'SICILY'

Rome

*Alban
Hills*

Anagni

CAMPAGNA

Marino

AND

MARITTIMA

Fondi

Miles

0 10 20 30 40 50

Terracina

THE STATES OF THE CHURCH IN ITALY
(after D. P. Waley, *The Papal State in the Thirteenth Century*)

had assuaged a pride which had been recently revived by Petrarch and Cola di Rienzo and a burst of prosperity. Urban V had shown that a pope's return was not necessarily lasting. It was well known that most of the cardinals longed to return, and that the king of France preferred the pope to be at Avignon. The election of a Limousin or French cardinal might well mean a return to the Rhône. The Roman mob naturally grew excited, and Romans were used to riots. The city's represenatives and the Roman nobility expressed Rome's desires to the cardinals, who could indeed hear them being shouted outside the Vatican: 'We want a Roman pope, or at least an Italian!'.

The election was somewhat hasty. As they could not agree among themselves on one of themselves, the cardinals decided to look outside the college. They were able to agree quickly that they would vote for an Italian, Bartolommeo Prignano, archbishop of Bari, whom they all knew well, since he had been Vice-Chancellor of the curia. But he could not be proclaimed before he had been accepted, and the crowd became excited by waiting and rumours spread. The bishop of Marseilles was warden of the conclave and he showed himself both foolish and weak-kneed, allowing in news and messengers, many of them with threats which alarmed and terrified the French cardinals in particular. They were frightened of the mob, and nervous that even a non-Roman Italian would not satisfy them and they organized a preposterous and foolish charade to calm the crowds. They presented them with one of the Roman cardinals, Cardinal Tebaldeschi, dressed up in the papal vestments. Prignano at last arrived and accepted and was generally recognized as pope. He took the name Urban VI and official announcements were sent out to princes and churchmen. He was crowned on Easter Sunday, April 18th, 1378.

It is quite undeniable that all the cardinals (bar one, who agreed to join the majority) agreed to elect Bartolommeo Prignano. It is equally undeniable that mob pressure, which had already made them choose an Italian, led them into striking follies. But all that would hardly have mattered if the new pope had behaved sensibly or even normally.

Urban VI, on the morrow of his election, showed himself to be coarse, rude and tactless to an extraordinary degree, unthinkable to those who had previously known him. He abused the cardinals, threw their wealth at them, and ordered the bishops in the curia back to their dioceses. He was startlingly rude to Charles V's favourite, Cardinal La Grange, who arrived after the election and was disappointed by it. The French cardinals were frightened of the Romans, and embittered by the pope's behaviour: they were afraid that there would be a great promotion of Italians to the college which would alter its balance. They began to hold meetings in which they recalled and discussed the difficulties and irregularities of Urban's election. It was plainly made under popular pressure—the presentation of Tebaldeschi to the crowd in papal dress proved that. Thirteen French cardinals left Rome for Anagni and refused to have any dealings with Urban VI. They denounced his election as 'null and void, not made freely, but under pressure', and after receiving a sympathetic letter from Charles V of France, they unanimously elected the Cardinal Robert of Geneva as pope on September 20th, 1378, at Fondi. He took the name 'Clement VII' and was crowned on All Saints' Day, November 1st.

'Clement VII's' election was notified to the world at large. Everywhere men puzzled and hesitated. Was a unanimous but pressurized election more lawful than one made five months later, out of Rome, and by a handful of cardinals only? The answers helped to split Christendom.

What made the split certain was the attitude of Charles V who declared for 'Clement'. In the lack of any clear religious division the split tended to be political: France and her allies one way, her enemies the other. The decisions of the princes were strong enough to carry local hierarchies and peoples. By 1379 there were two obediences. Round 'Clement' there rallied France, Sicily, Scotland, Castile, Aragon, Navarre, Portugal, Cyprus, Savoy and Irish Ireland: round 'Urban', England and Anglo-Ireland, Flanders, Poland, Hungary, Germany and central and northern Italy (where memories of the massacre of Cesena were still strong and so was anti-French feeling).

Both popes thought of Rome as the seat of the papacy. The man who held Rome would succeed. Urban was installed there, but Castel' Sant' Angelo was garrisoned by French mercenaries, and 'Clement' thought that he could use them and that with their support, that of Queen Joanna of Naples and a company of Breton mercenaries, he could seize the city. But Castel' Sant' Angelo surrendered on April 27th, 1379, and the Clementist forces were defeated at Marino on April 30th. 'Clement' had to retreat to Naples. But if Queen Joanna favoured him, popular sympathy was with the south Italian pope, Urban, who had been archbishop of Bari. 'Clement' was insecure in Naples and he gave up hope of an immediate conquest of Rome. He decided to go to the only papal town where he could live without difficulty, administer Christendom, and defeat the man whom he regarded as having usurped the Holy See—Avignon. 'Clement' left Naples on May 13th, 1379, with a good part of the court he had formed in Italy. He entered Avignon on June 20th, 1379.

★   ★   ★

For the third time, therefore, Avignon became a papal residence. But this time with a difference, for this pope was not the universally recognized Head of Christendom but a pope whom half of Christendom rejected, recognizing another in Rome. 'Clement VII' himself was certain of his position and so were his curia and the Christians who followed him: in their view he was the sole lawful pope, and the life of the papal court at Avignon was as it had been. However, the general attitude of the pope had changed—above all with regard to Rome. Rome was no longer the mystic bride of St. Peter's successor, the centre of an ideal Christendom where the pope would reside if he could and when circumstances permitted. Rome was now the seat of a rival pope, who pretended also to be the lawful pope; consequently it was the place where the Avignon pope wanted above all to be resident, for if he could establish himself there it would in itself be sufficient triumph. Avignon was no longer the stable residence of a pope in not too much hurry to return to Rome: however perfectly adapted Avignon might be to welcome 'Clement' and help him in his mission, it could only be the springboard for a pope determined to re-establish himself in Rome. The whole atmosphere was different. After the schism the Avignon popes did not have the placid confidence of their predecessors; they were more nervous and edgy; the palace-fortress they lived in became more symbolic of their position. Avignon might be the place where the pope lived, but it was quite plain that it was no longer the capital of Christendom.

'Clement VII' was the first of the Avignon popes who only governed a part of the Church. He was well-suited to these new circumstances.

He was the son of the count of Geneva and the countess of Boulogne and unlike his predecessors he was a member of a princely family, intermarried with most of the great families of Europe and closely related to the French king. He had entered the Church as a younger son and had moved rapidly up the ladder as canon of Paris, bishop of Thérouanne, then of Cambrai, before being made a cardinal by Gregory XI in 1371. As pope, he had the energy of a young man and the habits of a grand seigneur. He had presence and authority, he liked action, he had no scruples or difficulty when Gregory XI put him in charge of an army. Like a great nobleman, he was open-handed and splendid; he liked to patronize artists and men of letters and above all musicians and singers, as did the contemporary French princes. If 'Clement' had a programme he declared it in taking the name of Clement VI: it was his example that he would follow. His family connections made diplomacy easy for him—and it was on diplomacy and political manoeuvre that he relied for success.

Avignon suited him as a rallying point. It was in the absolute centre of the countries which obeyed him—near the counties of Geneva and Provence and the French and Spanish kingdoms, with easy connections by sea with Sicily and Cyprus, and with Italy, where his ambitions lay. It was an easy task to organize an administration. Gregory XI's government recognized his authority without too much difficulty and he was able to add the personnel that the devoted and competent papal Chamberlain, Pierre de Cros, had gathered together for him in Italy. By the end of June, 1379, the curia was functioning normally with a complete personnel, each department established in its usual quarters in the papal palace at Avignon.

'Clement VII's' policy was both Clement VI's and his own. He was a natural patron and he grouped round himself writers, humanists and artists. Their presence, like the great feasts and ceremonies which he promoted and increased made his court a brilliant one. Apart from personal taste there was a certain policy in this. The court at Avignon was as brilliant as that of most contemporary kings, if not more so, and appeared as the court of a great sovereign: its brilliance and importance made it quite clear that it was the true pope who lived at Avignon, not at Rome, where the unreliable and moody Urban VI drove men from his side with his coarseness and rudeness. To earthly and worldly glory God gave spiritual prestige. One of the first cardinals 'Clement' created was Peter of Luxembourg, to whom he gave the red hat under the canonical age, when he was only sixteen. Peter was a real saint and a genuinely holy young man. He died in 1387, worn out by his austerities and penances. Miracles and cures occurred at once at his tomb; crowds came on pilgrimage to Avignon, which received reflected sanctity. The earthly activity of this authentic saint coincided very happily with 'Clement VII's' pontificate. It was 'Clement' who made him a cardinal and his sanctity clearly justified making teenagers cardinals, taking bishops from princely families, and 'Clement's' own lawful possession of the papacy, for surely God would not so have blessed the entourage of an antipope?

The great object of 'Clement's' policy—as for all his predecessors, but with a difference—was to reconquer Italy, or at least Rome. He found ideal allies in the French princes who were trying to establish their kingdom in the south of Italy, the princes of the Capetian house of Anjou. Joanna I of Naples (1343–82) had designated Louis I of Anjou (Charles V's brother) as her heir to the kingdom of 'Sicily', i.e. Naples and the county of Provence. But Urban VI had invested her cousin Charles of

Durazzo and he was crowned at Naples. 'Clement VII' supported Louis spiritually and temporally, out of Church funds, and Louis's expedition to southern Italy in 1382—1384 had some success. He himself died in 1384, though, and his son, Louis II, who was heir to his rights, died in 1390. 'Clement' even thought of recreating the 'Kingdom of Adria' (invented by John XXII for John of Bohemia)[1] for Louis, Duke of Orleans, Charles VI's brother, who had married the daughter of Giangaleazzo Visconti. That was in 1393–4 and was to be in return for Orleans' assistance to 'Clement' in Italy. And to these great enterprises he added constant diplomatic activity, trying to persuade the Urbanist princes to recognize him as lawful pope. On the whole, and as a whole, he failed.

Patronage, court extravagance, war and diplomacy all cost money. 'Clement's' treasury was as empty as those of Urban V and Gregory XI, for all that he had no crusade and no Byzantine entanglements and worried about neither. Only constant borrowing and systematic and pitiless exaction of all the taxes levied by his predecessors on Church benefices kept him from disaster. He was lucky to have the richer of the two halves of Christendom to tax. France was the most populous and prosperous Western country in the fourteenth century. Despite forty years of war, ravaging and ruin, it had not lost all its wealth and 'Clement VII's' pontificate coincided with the economic revival which accompanied the victorious reign of Charles V. In 1378 nearly half the revenue of the Church came from France. France continued to subvent 'Clement' who, moreover, received his principal support from the French court and came very near, in 1390, to having an expedition led in person by Charles VI to Italy to restore him. He was not overworried by the complaints of a desperately overtaxed clergy.

Foreign policy in fact was not so very different under 'Clement VII' from what it had always been. But if he did live at Avignon much as his predecessors had done, he was always fretted and disturbed by the schism, which as far as he was concerned could only be solved by his presence at Rome.

[1] See p. 31 above.

Many even among his followers thought otherwise. They hoped that the schism, in itself a scandal and making for grave difficulties of conscience, while there might be no way of solving it in the lifetime of either pope, might be healed when one of them died. Urban VI's death in 1389 raised great hopes, but his cardinals did not, as was hoped, elect 'Clement' but one of themselves, who took the name Boniface IX.[1] 'Clement' himself died on September 16th, 1394, and the king of France, anxious to end the schism, tried to prevent the election of another pope; however, the conclave at Avignon, at the suggestion of the cardinal of Aragon, Pedro de Luna, refused to take cognisance of his message, which arrived after the conclave had begun. None the less, each cardinal took an oath to work for the extinction of the schism, even by abdicating the papacy if necessary if he were to be elected. Pedro de Luna was elected and he took the name 'Benedict XIII'.

Pedro de Luna was a member of a great Aragonese family. He had studied at Montpellier, where he had taught canon law, and he had obtained benefices in the churches of Cuença, Saragossa and Valencia. His knowledge, cultivation, wisdom and purity of life had all attracted Gregory XI's notice and it was Gregory who had made him a cardinal in 1375. He had weighed matters very carefully in 1378 before deciding which side to choose, but once having made up his mind he showed firmness and determination for 'Clement'. It was his diplomacy which had brought Castile, Aragon, Navarre and Portugal into 'Clement's' obedience. He had always shown great zeal for healing the schism, particularly during a long legation to the northern lands in 1392–4, when he had based himself on Paris.

He took up the Avignon succession at Avignon. He was no more a foreigner than 'Clement' had been: they were neither of them born in the French kingdom. 'Benedict XIII' was Aragonese—that is to say that he was a native of a country whose borders ran near Avignon and which had had great unsuccessful thirteenth-century ambitions for a political union

---

[1] For the succession of popes during the schism, see the appendix on pp. 136—7.

which would have embraced Languedoc and Provence in one great whole in which Avignon would have been included. His native language, Catalan, was very like that of the other popes from the Langue d'Oc, who had lived at Avignon since 1309. Although he tried to obtain the support of the kings of Aragon, whose Mediterranean Empire was now coming to its zenith and whose ambitions clashed with those of the French princes of the house of Anjou in Southern Italy, where they had been rivals for over a century, this does not entitle anyone to call him, as he has been called, a 'foreigner'. He had been both a student and a professor at Montpellier, and Avignon was on the edge of the countryside where he had spent his whole life.

The conditions of his election made his tenure of the papacy quite unlike that of any previous Avignon pope. His aim could not be the reconquest of Italy and Rome. That had been 'Clement's' principal aim; it could not be his: circumstances were altered. He had, however, sufficient wit and diplomatic skill to enter into all the projects and plans—not to say dreams—which would ensure him the support of Louis of Orleans, Charles VI's brother, to whom he continued to promise an Italian kingdom, part of it to be cut out of the states of the Church. The real problem for 'Benedict' was his personal role in ending the schism. Christendom would not tolerate permanent partition and neither pope had been able to depose the other by force. The best thinkers, scholars and royal counsellors of the day occupied their minds with the problem of the schism: neither of the two colleges of cardinals had found an end to the schism either at the death of 'Clement VII' or at that of Urban VI; now it was the task of the kings and bishops, the leaders of the various peoples and the faithful themselves to find some solution to a situation which all Christians found insupportable. The University of Paris, the theological centre of Christendom, proposed the 'way of cession': that is, that both popes should resign. And the same solution was called for, and adopted, by a large assembly of prelates and prominent laymen of the kingdom of France called together by Charles VI in 1395. As 'Benedict' had promised that he would resign the papacy if the interest of the Church required it, before he was elected, the king of France now asked that he should do so.

'Benedict XIII' then adopted the attitude of polite but firm refusal which, as a result of his obstinacy and longevity, was the principal cause of prolonging the schism. As pope he kept his sense of the deep meaning and grandeur of the pope's office, a dignity higher than any other on earth, which makes him who is invested with it vicar of God; and no man may, if he would, lay down *that* charge. His idea of the papacy had all the grandeur of notions of theocracy and *plenitudo potestatis*. 'Benedict XIII' brought to the papacy the same deep pride in his office that Boniface VIII had brought to it. To support a doctrine he felt so intensely he had the resources of an admirably learned canonist, a truly masterly diplomat, a physically brave and mulishly obstinate Spanish nobleman and a deeply religious and pure-living man, whose genuine piety was underlined by the holiness of his confessor and compatriot, St. Vincent Ferrer. He was capable, and he showed it, of persevering if necessary alone against all in the name of the office to which God had called him and which it was not for him to abandon.

He denied that either the University of Paris, or the King of France, or the cardinals who agreed with the king of France (sometimes not very disinterestedly), had any of them any right to advise a pope to resign, an unthinkable suggestion; or to appeal from the present pope to his uncontested successor. He deceived their impatience by negotiations with the pope in Rome which he knew very well would come to nothing. To the threats of the king of France that he would allow no more clerical taxation to come to Avignon, he sought refuge in support from the king of Aragon and in a personally austere life.

The general assembly of the French clergy denounced him as a 'creator and fosterer of schism' and asked the king to withdraw obedience from him, to force him to give way, and to make him resign. The king withdrew the French obedience on July 27th, 1398. All the cardinals save five deserted him at once, carrying off his very seal, the majority of the curia left the palace, and, roused by their bishops, the people of Avignon and the Comtat Venaissin rose against him. 'Benedict XIII' impassively shut himself up in the papal palace with a handful of servants who were faithful to him and two hundred Catalan soldiers—and Benedict XII's and Clement VI's great fortress showed itself when commanded by a man of his temper to be indeed what Froissart had called it: 'the most beautiful and the strongest house in the world, and the easiest to defend.' The cardinals and the king of France did not hesitate to hire an entirely villainous mercenary commander, Geoffrey de Boucicaut, to attack the palace. Just as he had defied his general betrayal, so 'Benedict' refused to give way to siege and resisted it manfully from October, 1398 to April, 1399. For six months he was at every weak point to encourage his troops and devise stratagems to foil the enemy; and he triumphed. He compelled admiration. The scandal of besieging a pope distressed men's consciences, and the diplomacy of the king of Aragon eventually obtained the concession of compromise: 'Benedict XIII' should live in the palace under the guard of the duke of Orléans and should not leave it without the authorization of the king of France. Even if his residence at Avignon was now enforced 'Benedict' was still pope; he had carried his point with uncommon energy and time was on his side.

Naturally, these affairs occupied all his energies, they left him no time for the East. Luck would have it that just as there was a Catalan pope the Catalan duchy of Athens should fall into the hands of the Florentines in alliance with the Anjou kings of Southern Italy. If 'Benedict' had been pope six years earlier, if he had had time or money, he might have helped his countrymen. But no Christian power in the Balkans could now hope to stop the victorious progress of the Turks who were now masters of Bulgaria and Greece after their great triumph at the battle of Kossovo. Only a major expedition from the West might do it, and such an expedition was urgent. 'Benedict XIII', however, had nothing to do with it. It was the count of Nevers, Philip the Bold's son, and Charles VI's first cousin, who organized it with the blessing of the Roman Pope, Boniface IX.

It ended with the tragic disaster of Nicopolis in 1396, which demonstrated yet again that without the joint action of the French and English kings nothing was to be hoped for in the East.

'Benedict XIII' did not long administer the Church of his obedience since there was very little of it left after 1398, when the kingdoms of France, Sicily, Castile, Navarre and the County of Provence were all removed from it. Rome was always considered the capital of the Christian world and its prestige drew away Christians of the Avignonese obedience. Despite prohibitions from kings the Jubilee of 1400 drew crowds of French and Spanish pilgrims to the tombs of the apostles and such crowds showed by the mere fact of their pilgrimage the esteem in which they held Avignon where their lawful pope lived, for all its new shrines.

Thus it was that for four years and six months, from 1398 to 1403, 'Benedict XIII' lived at Avignon, virtually a prisoner in his inviolate palace. Then, in the night either of March 11th or March 12th, 1403, he escaped in disguise and took refuge in the lands of the count of Provence. Shortly afterwards various kings gave way to his tenacity and restored their obedience.

But 'Benedict XIII' never returned to Avignon. He led a life of frequent moves from place to place in Provence, Languedoc and Roussillon, his obstinacy continuously obstructing all attempts at ending the schism. Finally he was deposed at the council of Constance in 1415. But he did not accept this unthinkable deposition of a pope. He retired to an inaccessible rocky peninsula, to Peñiscola in Catalonia, and, defying the world which forgot him, died, still pope, in 1422, aged ninety-four.

No later pope ever resided at Avignon. The memories of the schism went some way to discredit it. But hopes remained tenacious. When Martin V, the sole pope who emerged from the council of Constance, had still not firmly decided to settle at Rome, in 1420, there were those hopeful persons who thought he might come back to the Rhône. Twenty years later there was a possibility that the council of Basel might come to

Avignon, near the sea and in easy communication with the East, so that it could work for the union of the churches, but such hopes evaporated.

After having sheltered the popes one way or the other for ninety-four years Avignon ceased to be a papal residence at the beginning of the fifteenth century. There are two clear periods to be distinguished in those ninety-four years. The first runs from 1309 to 1376 when Avignon, as the residence of the sole pope, was the undoubted capital of Christendom; the second, from 1379 to 1403, when it was only the centre of half Christendom. But the life of the papal court—at least till 1398—continued much as it had been during the first period and this century of the popes' stay is the high point of Avignon's history.

That century made Avignon an international capital. It had its consequences for the Church, too, however, for its life and government, and indeed, for the life and civilization of Western Christendom.

V

Avignon as the Home of the Papal Curia and as the Capital of Christendom

Clement V had on the whole preferred Avignon to any of the towns of the Comtat Venaissin which belonged to the Church. John XXII preferred it much more. Their successors installed themselves firmly there and, finally, after the sale of the city, held it in full sovereignty. The conditions of existence and work in Avignon affected the work and activity of the pope and curia for sixty-seven years, and had perceptible influence on the structure and evolution of the papal court, as on the administration of the Church which grew up at Avignon just at the highly important period in which the governmental and administrative system of the thirteenth-century popes achieved its final form.

*   *   *

Avignon was at the beginning of the fourteenth century one of the largest towns of the Rhône valley, much more important than those of the neighbouring Comtat Venaissin, though not large by twentieth-century standards.

There were still some remains of the town's Roman period when it had been of moderate importance. It was the seat of a bishopric, but dioceses were numerous in Provence, as in Italy, which made a bishopric a less important and smaller affair than it would be in the North, and the diocese was small and so were the bishop's revenues. However, in the twelfth century, thanks to the new flour and fulling mills on the banks of the river Sorgue, Avignon had a mild economic boom which expressed itself in a charter from the count of Provence giving the town a consulate (a magistrature), and by the building of walls with a circumference of nearly two miles, about 130–150 feet high, a good deal bigger than the walls it inherited from the later Roman Empire. The last and most important sign of this prosperity was the building of the famous bridge, the Pont St. Bénézet.

In the thirteenth century the town grew more slowly. Its walls were destroyed as a result of a siege by Louis VIII in 1226 (campaigning against the Albigensians) and later in the century Charles of Anjou decreed that they should not be rebuilt. But in order to get more power for the mills a tributary of the Durance, the Durançole, was diverted into the Sorgue. The only important building (apart from what happened to every town, houses for each of the four orders of Friars and a convent of Poor Clares) was the university, founded by Boniface VIII at the request of King Charles II of 'Sicily' in 1303. It had only two faculties—arts and canon law.

The town had eight parishes including the cathedral, Notre Dame des Doms; it had three monasteries and a Templar commandery. The consuls were recruited from the nobility, though the nobles had little power. Despite their fortified houses in which they lived even inside the city itself they were not remotely comparable in power to the great Roman barons with their big country fiefs and estates. The populace do not seem to have been very turbulent. The basic material is lacking for population figures in 1300, but taking other towns for which the figures are known a rough estimate can be made and the population cannot have been larger, if as large as 5,000–6,000 inhabitants. This was a middle-sized town for the time. It possessed advantages which contributed to its rise: the natural fortress of the cathedral rock, the Rocher des Doms, and a position where the Rhône ran through two outcrops of limestone, and its situation on the Rhône valley, discussed in an earlier chapter. It was a natural place to build a bridge and, once built, the bridge served to increase its importance. The water of the Sorgue had meant the rise of a variety of small industries and the university meant the beginnings of an intellectual life.

These are the advantages which are likely to have led the popes to have preferred Avignon to one of the small towns of the Comtat Venaissin—for example, Carpentras. The other important element was the climate. In summer, the popes could move very easily and comfortably into papal territory and enjoy cooler air at the cost of a very slight rise in sea level. Avignon and the Comtat Venaissin are very different from Rome, which nowadays becomes intolerable in summer (and it was even more so in the Middle Ages), and must be left because of the hot, unhealthy weather which has killed so many northern popes. In summer at Rome the popes had to move into the Alban or Sabine hills, or to the shores of Lake Bracciano. Anagni, Rieti, Viterbo or Montefiascone are all thirty-five miles from Rome. Sorgues, Noves and Châteauneuf are only twelve miles from Avignon. The popes never went into neighbouring Provence or Dauphiné. Exceptionally, the Black Death in Clement VI's time, and the foundation of a Charterhouse in Innocent VI's, sent Avignon popes over the Rhône into France to spend a few days at Villeneuve-les-Avignon, in the lands of the French king. The enervating gusts of the *mistral* can be trying, but otherwise the summer climate of Avignon is excellent, the popes never had to move far from Avignon for summer refreshment and so the curia could be left behind when they did. The small size of the Comtat Venaissin, its little hills and gentle summers all meant a stable order for the administration of the Church, which could remain all the year round in Avignon itself. Such stability had never been possible when the pope was in the Lateran and the unhealthy Roman summers drove him to the distant hills. The popes lived on the banks of the Rhône in conditions very different from those they had known on the banks of the Tiber—in so far as their predecessors ever had lived there. They had nothing to fear from the people of Avignon who had no local traditions of civic greatness or mob rule, were not in fact numerous and had no great or powerful noble families to be represented in the sacred college by influential cardinals. The popes had nothing to fear from outside attack on the Rocher des Doms, where their fortress was impregnable, and they had no need to move out of it or to move their administration about: health and climate compensated for the small size of the Comtat Venaissin and there was no need to go outside it. The natural conditions in Avignon, to sum up, made the papacy secure, stable and sedentary.

★   ★   ★

The fixed abode of the popes at Avignon meant that their court could and did grow, as is clear from the steady extension of the palace.

The papal court was constituted by all those persons who helped the pope to govern and administer the Church, those who surrounded him to protect and honour him and those who were a cross between the two. Their number increased steadily as the pope assumed the direction of Christendom and the increase of trade permitted the provisioning of great collections of people with necessities and luxuries. Already towards the end of the thirteenth century Nicholas III's court was two hundred and ten people. The magnificence and nepotism of Boniface VIII raised the number to more than three hundred. But up to 1316 the popes led a semi-nomadic existence and this in itself prevented the growth of the curia.

As soon as the curia settled down at Avignon, in a palace where the various departments never had to shift and where they became more and more organized, it was able to develop in an orderly and progressive way without any kind of restraint. As the papal civil service stopped wandering so they stopped being paid in kind. From 1310 Clement V made wage payments in cash and that moment marks the opening of the modern era in papal administration.

The papal court included the pope's own household, the college of cardinals—who together with the pope are the government of the Church—the administrative and judicial services of the Church, the guards, ceremonial officials, and the palace functionaries.

83

Avignon as the Home of the Papal Curia

1. The Pope's Household are those of his near relations who live with him, the officials who assist at his prayers, serve his chapel, look after his health, look after his vestments and regalia and dust his rooms: chaplains, doctors, chamberlains, several dozens of people. But their number was always increasing. For example, there was a need for someone to take care of the ornaments and *objets d'art* which the pope was constantly being presented with —those, that is, which were not stored in the treasury. Then there was a need for librarians, for the papal library grew much larger (it is one of the most striking features of the stay at Avignon and was due to the fact that the popes were not moving about). The library came to occupy the time of a staff of specialist secretaries and chaplains.

2. The Sacred College, as such, only meant the cardinals and the college's very few officials, of whom the Cardinal Chamberlain was the most important. The Camera or Chamber of the college of cardinals received from the Camera Apostolica that share of the Church's revenues which went to the cardinals and which was shared among them. The cardinals gathered around the pope in Consistory in a special room of the papal palace. But they lived outside the palace in houses of their own, each with their own 'livery' or 'hotel' and a considerable body of servants as befitted princes of the Church. The chaplains, secretaries, gentlemen and other servants of a cardinal formed his 'familia' or household. The senior member of such a household would be the auditor, who heard cases brought before the cardinal's court. A cardinal's 'familia' was a miniature of the papal court: it was never less than twenty people and often rose to fifty.

3. The Administrative and Judicial Departments of the Church, which were the Camera Apostolica, the Chancery, the various courts and the Penitentiary. They were all housed in the palace.

A. *The Camera Apostolica* dealt with papal finances. The Chamberlain who directed it often went further and took part in financial diplomacy. In effect he was the pope's Finance Minister and his Foreign Minister. The second in command was the Papal Treasurer whose business it was to look after the treasury, keep the accounts, register income and expenditure. The Chamberlain and Treasurer were assisted by five clerks of the Chamber, by notaries, couriers, writing-clerks, and by a legal staff who served the court of the Camera, before which came many financial matters. The Mint and its officials were at Sorgues till 1348, when they moved to Avignon. In either place they were under the Chamberlain's authority.

B. *The Chancery* was a collection of departments which dealt with papal correspondence. At its head was the Vice-Chancellor. The most important departments dealt with the secret letters, but as nominations to benefices by the popes grew, the correspondence dealing with benefices grew larger. Once the request or supplication of a candidate for a benefice—generally brought by a procurator—had been approved and signed by the pope, it had to be registered by the Board of Supplications; the Board of Examinations must assure itself of his fitness; the Board of Inscriptions drew up the letter which conferred the benefice; the Board of Engrossment put it into form; the Board of the Collector collated the engrossment; the Board of Seals sealed it; and the Board of Registration registered it. The process occupied more than a hundred notaries and writing-clerks.

C. *The Papal Tribunals* each had a staff of auditors and advocates. The highest was the Consistory composed of the pope and cardinals, and in theory it heard all cases and appeals. But since innumerable cases were reserved to the pope's jurisdiction and it was clearly impossible to judge them all, the Consistory delegated certain cases to the cardinals' courts which then instructed it, leaving to the Consistory or the pope himself the final decision. The Consistory had also got rid of all cases relating to benefices which went to the Court of Audience of the papal palace—normally known as the Rota, because its auditors sat on a circular bench. The Rota gave judgment without appeal on all cases sent to it by the pope and Vice-Chancellor. Before being introduced before the Rota many cases came before the Court of Audience of Contradictory Letters which dealt with objections of a technical nature made by one of the parties to a suit.

D. *The Papal Penitentiary* really was a spiritual tribunal. In the pope's name it gave canonical dispensations, lifted ecclesiastical censures, dealt with irregularities in the life of the clergy and absolved the sins specially reserved for the pope's absolution. It was directed by the cardinal who held the post of Grand Penitentiary, who was assisted by twelve lesser penitentiaries (normally friars), and a dozen writing-clerks.

4. The Guards and Ceremonial Officers looked after the guarding of the pope, the inside and outside guard of the palace and were the pope's escort when he moved about or in ceremonies. There were knights and noble squires, porters and sergeants-at-arms. Their numbers tended to vary with the tastes of any given pope for personal display, but they gradually came to be about two hundred persons.

5. The Palace Staff: there were four basic departments: kitchen, pantry, buttery and marshalsea (the stables), which between them looked after the pope's meals and moves, the meals of those who ate in the palace, the papal messengers and the palace generally. The almonery should be added, which each day fed a hundred poor men; and also there should be added the staff of odd-job men, gardeners, and those who kept the palace in repair.

Each of these departments in the papal court tended to increase with the course of time, with the development of the pope's power in the Church at large and the state kept by the sovereign pontiff. Inevitably the whole increased and inflated with the pope's stay at Avignon, for the sedentary nature of that stay favoured increase.

On the average there must have been about five hundred papal officials. Despite the building of two successive palaces side by side to accommodate the various departments they could not all fit inside: neither the almonery proper, where the alms were actually distributed, nor the department of the seal, which was part of the chancery, nor the mint, were ever there, and various kitchen departments and the marshalsea were, like them, housed in unfurnished lodgings hired in the town. These higgledy-piggledy arrangements alone show the rapid unplanned increase of the papal court which the palace built to contain it could not, in fact, contain, and show too the absence of logic and central direction in the divisions of departments and business inside the palace. Most of the officials took lodgings in the town; and as well as the pope's officials there were the staffs of the cardinals: thirty persons at least, each, for twenty-three cardinals means nearly a thousand people. (With five hundred papal officials that gives us fifteen hundred.) But two-thirds of all these were laymen—a thousand or so laymen. The clergy directed all departments and held the basic offices and the clergy were never under the orders of the laity. These thousand laymen, though, had often enough families of their own, wives, children, dependants, all living in the town. So the whole total of papal and cardinals' staffs with hangers-on was probably about three thousand souls.

These officials came from all over Christendom. But most of the Avignon popes came from southern France and practised nepotism. A hundred and thirteen of the hundred and thirty-four cardinals created between 1309 and the schism in 1378 were Frenchmen, and three-quarters of those came from the Langue d'Oc. Consequently a large proportion of the curia and the 'families' of the various cardinals came from the Langue d'Oc too. Men from Gascony, the Limousin or Quercy (and Catalans and Aragonese as well), could easily understand the Provençal which was the native language in Avignon. The core of the papal court was from the Langue d'Oc. It is not precisely incorrect to say, 'all Avignon popes were Frenchmen', because all of those before 'Clement VII' were born in the kingdom of France, and several of them knew or had served the French king before becoming pope. But it is more correct to say that they were popes of the Langue d'Oc (Mediterranean, southern France—which is not the France of the Île de France or Normandy—Langue d'Oil, where 'oui' means 'yes'). They, their friends and relations and officials, were naturally adapted to Avignon, to its climate, language and way of life. The very saints honoured in the town were those of the Langue d'Oc: all the men of the Limousin who came with Clement VI, Innocent

87

VI and Gregory XI had St. Martial of Limoges as their patron
and brought the cult of that apostle of Aquitaine with them;
Clement VI dedicated one of the chapels in the palace to him
and Androin de la Roche, abbot of Cluny, dedicated his college
for monks in Avignon to St. Martial.

It was both numbers and local connections which made an
all but insurmountable difficulty in going back to Rome. The
larger the staff, the more difficult the move—it was logistically
unprecedented, appallingly expensive and upsetting and without contemporary parallel. The sedentary court suffered from
fat and hardening of the arteries: a move meant a serious dis-
turbance and dislocation of all its functions. Moreover, the
great majority of the curia could only view a move to Rome as
exile from their native land. The fact that the curia was so
unwilling made the practical difficulties so much the greater. It
took superhuman willpower and the strongest spiritual motiva-
tion to heave the curia from Avignon in 1367 and 1376.

★   ★   ★

Avignon, like other towns on which the papal court descended
in its nomad days—like Vienne when the Council came to it—
might have been crushed by the enormous weight which fell on
it. In fact this was not so: it never really found the burden insupportable—even at first. The reasons are various. First comes
the fact that Clement V's court which arrived in 1309 was still
the court of an itinerant pope. It was only in John XXII's time
that the court became sizeable and by then the town had had
time to accustom itself to the pope's presence and to increase
as the court increased. Then again, Avignon was a fairly important town, not a cathedral village like Vienne or Carpentras,
and the large working-class with its very varied activities, the
farm lands round about and the neighbouring countryside, were
all capable of provisioning and furnishing the court. Finally,
since most of the court came from much the same part of France
and spoke Provençal, they did not seem like real foreigners to
a population who did not think of them as extortionate or op-
pressive. These fortunate accidents explain why there was never

any hostility between the town of Avignon and the papal court. On the contrary, this little town with its calm and charm, without any haughty pretensions or difficult nobles, delighted by its unhoped-for prosperity, was the ideal place for the papal court to relax and expand with a sense of ease. Avignon grew to accommodate the papal court *'avec ravissement'*.

The only real difficulty was about lodgings, because the curia and cardinals needed too many unfurnished ones. A committee had to be appointed to list, tax and allot them. The problem continued to exist all through the century because even when the building programme came abreast of the court's increase so that every official had a roof over his head, there was still a great crowd of visitors.

Within a few years Avignon was a big city. The presence of the pope, the sacred college and the curia, and the visits to them of all the prelates of Christendom made it a religious centre. There were exceptionally magnificent ceremonies, fifty-eight major liturgical feasts annually, plus Sundays, plus the special festivities for canonizations, the despatch of the Golden Rose to a selected Christian prince on the last Sunday in Lent, the reception of ambassadors, Christian, schismatic and pagan. Perhaps the most moving ceremony of all was the papal blessing given to the pressing crowds below from the great Gothic window beside the papal chapel. Popes, cardinals, prelates, founded churches, chapels, monasteries and gave new endowments to old ones; the churches of St. Peter and St. Desiderius were rebuilt and enlarged; and the friaries of the Dominicans and Cordeliers were transformed, thanks to the innumerable rich gifts made by princes of the Church anxious to have the intercession of Poverty (vicarious) at the Last Judgment. In Urban V's time a Benedictine nunnery and a Benedictine college were both founded—the latter for monk students to attend the university. The sanctity of St. Peter of Luxembourg made Avignon a pilgrimage centre, and 'Clement VII' founded a house of Celestines to protect and honour the shrine.

This great burgeoning of religious establishments and rich foundations turned Avignon into a colossal building site as well as a centre of learning. The town became an artistic centre to which architects, sculptors, painters, and all sorts of minor artists came, avid for patronage. They came from all countries, but many of them, above all the architects, came from the Langue d'Oc like most of the prelates who employed them.

At the same time Avignon became an important intellectual centre. The fourteenth-century clergy were intellectuals. Amongst the papal court itself there were men who were eminent scholars, and there was a constant flow, sometimes for long stays, of visitors and petitioners, among them prelates and scholars from all over Christendom who contributed to a strong concentration of learned men.

The university of Avignon offered a chance for all candidates for benefices to better their qualifications, the humbler ones by attending some part of the ten-year course which led to the doctorate, the more eminent by taking chairs; and sometimes very eminent men did so. The teaching of a great civil lawyer like Baldo degli Ubaldi or the great Bologna canon lawyer John of Legnano must have made a considerable impression. For scholars, papal provision to benefices was their chief hope, and they could hope for more from the pope's disinterested patronage than they could from that of kings or bishops.

Law, canon or civil, was what flourished at this university, which existed in the context of the men who were collecting the most recent decretals (papal judgments which would form new precedents in canon law) in the collections which were called the *Clementines* and the *Extravagantes* (i.e. those issued by Clement V and those extra to, and going beyond, the great thirteenth-century compilations of the law of the Church). The arts faculty was nothing more than a preparatory school for the law faculty and arts graduates who came to Avignon did not bother to attend it. The medical faculty could not bear comparison with the very celebrated neighbouring medical faculty at Montpellier, and the great doctors in any case tended to be recruited from the southern French Jews. What is peculiarly striking is that there was *no* faculty of theology at the university of Avignon in papal times—the university's theology faculty was founded in 1413. The crown of study in Avignon was the doctorate in one of the two laws and it was held by many of the curia and the papal officials.

Papal centralization involved the calling of many cases to Avignon, particularly those concerning benefices. Papal temporal policy involved complex legal questions. Both gave canon and civil lawyers a chance to shine. The schism, far from reducing such activity, did much to increase it, with ceaseless discussion and new arguments to be refuted. The use of the papal library and those of the cardinals was freely given and the university library was very greatly improved, particularly by legacies from cardinals early in the fifteenth century. From 1380 onwards the court of the titular king of Sicily was at Aix-en-Provence reasonably near by, so that a common policy could be worked out for pope and king in Italy; and it had a staff of civil lawyers, many of them priests.

Many of these clerks in minor orders and priests, papal secretaries, royal counsellors, princely advisers, notaries and so on were themselves interested in literature and *belles-lettres*, and wrote elegant and evocative prose, and even verse, in a style very different from that of their official correspondence and memoranda. The greatest was Petrarch, son of a papal notary, whose life—he was born in 1304 and died in 1374—almost exactly covered that stay of the popes in Avignon which he denounced so bitterly. Chance would have it that this worshipper of Rome would do more than any other man for the future fame of Avignon by writing his poetry there, in particular his immortal sonnets to Laura. But in his lifetime it was not his Italian verse which made Petrarch famous at Avignon. It was his writings and letters in Latin in which he laid the foundations and defined the aims of Renaissance humanism. From his example, both in his lifetime and after his death, a certain number of cosmopolitan literary men, both clergy and laity, researched into, studied and imitated classical Latin. Like Petrarch, they had no Greek. Such were Giovanni Moccia from Naples, Jean Muret from Maine, Robert Burgundion the Cistercian and Nicholas of Clamanges from Champagne, all of whom were secretaries to 'Clement VII' and 'Benedict XIII', and made up a small circle of friends who wrote topical verses, epitaphs and love lyrics on ancient models with classical quotations and pagan allusions. Their language was Latin. Latin, whether ecclesiastical or Ciceronian, whether legal or literary, was the language of Avignon, the universal speech used and loved as a common *lingua franca* by Frenchmen of northern France, Frenchmen of the Langue d'Oc and Italians.

*   *   *

This crowd of residents, visitors and petitioners had to be fed, housed and lodged and provided with what their often lengthy purses could buy. Avignon, under the pressure of the needs of the papal court and its clustering clergy became an active industrial centre, an important regional market and a centre of international commerce.

All the surrounding plains and valleys increased their products of cereals, wine, fruit and vegetables: the lower Alps were increasingly cultivated, from the Atlantic coast (mainly) there was imported the large supply of fish necessary to a large clerical population, the Alpine forests provided timber for all the new building and local manufactures grew generally with demand. Avignon itself had not a sufficiently large commercial class for this expanded trade. The Jews were given papal protection. There were about two hundred families of Jews in the town, mostly engaged in industry and local trade. Above all, there was a great influx of country folk and villagers from the valleys of the Saône and Rhône, especially of the poverty-stricken mountain people from the Alps, who came to settle in the town, to work on the building sites or in the clothes and food trades.

But since the richest benefice holders in Christendom either lived permanently in or came for a time to Avignon, the town was a place where some of the richest men in the world were to be found. They needed to be able to transfer funds and change currency and they also wanted luxuries apart from those to be obtained locally—the great wines of Beaune and St. Pourçain-sur-Sioule. There was a splendid market for the great international merchants. These were not, as is so often said, the Jews, who, as I have mentioned, were purely local traders, but almost exclusively Italians, citizens of the most active trading cities in the world, and especially Tuscans. The great size and international links of the Florentine trading companies and merchant banks, the traditional attachment of Florence to the Guelf alliance, of which the head was the pope, while the French king of Sicily and count of Provence was its chief military prop—all these things meant that the Florentine companies had every reason and inducement to open branches at Avignon which were soon among their most prosperous and active. These banks would change currency, or transfer funds to anywhere in Christendom; they took deposits and made loans, often on security of jewellery; they imported silks, gold thread, eastern spices, furs and precious metals from the Baltic, cloth from Flanders and Florence, French linen and *objets d'art*. Their presence, which was the result of that of the curia, made Avignon one of the great commercial and banking centres of Christendom. It totally eclipsed nearby Marseilles and Nîmes, and practically extinguished Montpellier.

Thus by its presence and activity the papal court had rapidly changed the medium-sized town on the Rhône into a great city, full of clergy, merchants and soldiers, to which came, more than to any other city, prelates, princes, and kings from every country. Its population went on rising: to the original inhabitants of 1300 there were added immigrant workmen and traders both from the locality and from far-off countries. Workmen, traders and courtiers or officials made up a population of about 30,000 in 1376. That means that Avignon was one of the great cities of the West. It would not bear comparison with the great trading towns of neighbouring Italy, Venice, Genoa, Florence, Milan or Naples; but in France only Paris (which then had a good 100,000 inhabitants) surpassed it easily. It was as important as big Low Country towns like Bruges and London and Rouen. Much more than any trading city it always had at any time a great floating population of visitors and petitioners to fill its numerous inns and taverns. It was a very big town,

The building of the third set of walls between 1360 and 1370 showed how much it had grown: the circumference was about two and two-third miles, enclosing an area more than three times that inside the previous set of walls. In France, only the walls of Paris surrounded so wide an area.

Avignon was a capital city. In the fourteenth century the various specialized sections of the royal courts—great legal bodies like the Parlements (or, e.g., the Court of King's Bench), treasuries like the Chambre des Comptes (or the Exchequer)—did not move about the country as they once had; kings built great palaces where they could live for long periods in the midst of the brilliant courts which were paid for by heavy taxes; kings favoured too the rise of universities near their palaces, which would provide them with the lawyers, the lay and ecclesiastical administrators they needed. Such juxtaposition of courts and universities meant centres of conspicuous consumption which drew international merchants who had previously followed fairs; kings built walls round such cities to protect themselves, their governments, the universities and the merchants—the large communities that their very presence drew to such cities and which made them so rich. Avignon was such a city and could be compared to the greatest capitals in the West.

Like Naples under the kings of the house of Anjou, like Paris under the Valois, like Prague under Charles IV, Avignon was a great capital city. But its court was exceptional in its nature; it was not, like Naples or Paris or Prague the capital of a kingdom. That was what made it unique.

It was the capital of a state with no real temporal basis, the capital of an international power, the capital of Christendom, or, as Petrarch furiously called it, 'the capital of the world': the only international centre of the West, and the only conceivable international centre. The cardinals who governed it, the clergy who lived there, the merchants who worked there, were of all nationalities, like the mercenaries who guarded it. Its tiny original population was swallowed in the vast international immigration. Even the population of Avignon was cosmopolitan. The town's initial comparative unimportance, its absence of pretension and tradition served it well, as did its exceptional situation as the city to which all the roads of Christendom actually did leave. Avignon gave the papacy which desperately needed it a place where it could stop moving about, something that it was becoming both more difficult and damaging to do, as the papacy collected staff and equipment: a place where it could become sedentary in safety, as were the great national administrations of contemporary kings.

In return the papacy made Avignon prosperous and glorious.

VI

Avignon and the Centralization of the Church

Avignon, as a site where the papacy could be established in stability, in a convenient centre where dealings were easy with all parts of Christendom, where a great palace could be built and the curia developed, was, as a result, a place where the centralization of the Church under papal authority developed to a high point which it had never previously reached and which is the first great landmark in that development.

Since Gregory VII's time, in the eleventh century, the popes had firmly taken the moral leadership of Christendom and under Urban II at the end of the century they had taken the general direction of Christendom on themselves by sponsoring the crusade: and their influence over clergy and laity grew steadily and was constantly reinforced. Centralization of the Church had grown with papal prestige and better communications. Its justification lay in the words of Christ to St. Peter when He made him shepherd of his flock ('Feed my lambs, feed my sheep'). From the Petrine texts flowed the pope's primacy of jurisdiction and the thirteenth-century canonists had progressively deduced a teaching on the pope's supremacy in the Church which affected the interior life of the Church quite as much as its relations with the State. The pope's 'plenitude of power' had internal as well as external application.

These claims to a greater and greater effective government of the whole Church showed themselves in three otherwise separate areas: in nominations to benefices—that is, the direct appointment of clergy to ecclesiastical offices (parishes, canon-

ries and bishoprics) all over Christendom; in the imposition of
papal taxes on holders of benefices (whether papally appointed
or not); and the increasingly monarchical nature of the Church's
constitution. In all three areas of government the Avignon popes
made considerable advances. They were all canon lawyers and
frequently civil lawyers as well. These three areas must each be
treated in turn.

First, *benefices*. Benefices were commonly divided into two
categories, major and minor. Major benefices were bishoprics
and abbeys. Minor benefices were canonries, posts in cathedral
chapters, archpresbyteries,[1] rural deaneries, parishes, chaplaincies, priories. Minor benefices were again divided into those
which carried cure of souls (like parishes) and those which did
not and which were therefore styled *sine cura*, without cure of
souls, sinecures. The classic type of the second kind of minor
benefice was a canonry. By the thirteenth century the Gregorian
Reform had accomplished many of its objectives and the normal
way of appointment to a major benefice was election (canons
elected bishops, monks elected abbots). The normal way of
appointment to a minor benefice was nomination. Bishops
named men to canonries, archpresbyteries or deaneries. *Patrons*
named men to parishes and chaplaincies. Patrons could be laymen or churchmen, depending on by whom, when and how,
the respective parish churches or chapels had been founded
or endowed.[2]

If, with a major benefice, an election was contested, arbitration was sought. The frequent appearances of papal legates all
over Christendom since Gregory VII's time tended to lessen the
importance of archbishops or metropolitans and therefore such
arbitration became more and more the province of the pope,
and his primacy of jurisdiction meant that there was no further
appeal from his decisions (which made them attractive).

Such interventions in elections meant that popes increased

---

[1] Translator's note. A 'dean' in Continental Europe is often called an
'archpriest'. It means the head of a large, normally collegiate, church.

[2] Translator's note. Lay patronage was an important piece of private
property and the popes tended to interfere with it less.

their influence by nominating to particular bishoprics and they sought to multiply opportunity. In 1265 with the bull *Licet Ecclesiarum*, Clement IV formulated the principle which made such nominations systematic and regular. In virtue of the pope's primacy of jurisdiction as successor of St. Peter and supreme Head of the Church, instituted as such by Christ Himself, the pope had, if he wished, full disposal of all benefices and cures of souls.

Such a principle could hardly be immediately or generally applied. Late thirteenth-century popes applied it above all to those cases where the holder had died in the curia or in its immediate neighbourhood (these were called benefices *vacantes in curia*). The Avignon popes applied it more frequently and generally. They had recourse to a number of procedures. The simplest was nomination or 'provision' by *mandate*, which consisted in the pope's naming, in a case where the nomination was contested, clerk A to benefice B. The second, and most effective, one was *reservation*: he reserved all appointments to a certain category or kind of benefice in a given Church, province or kingdom, or even in all Christendom, to himself; and he might do this for all the benefices of a particular cleric newly deceased or all the benefices of a particular church ('special reservation'). The third was the process of appointment by *expectation*, used for minor benefices, where the pope gave an order to the patron who would normally appoint to give clerk A the next benefice of such and such a category which became vacant in his gift (for example, to a bishop, to give clerk A the next vacant canonry in his cathedral). Fourth, the pope could, for major benefices, use his exclusive right of *translation*, that of permitting the transfer of bishops from one diocese to another, thus over-riding the rights of the cathedral chapters.

By the easy use and variation of these methods the Avignon popes little by little multiplied their powers and the use they made of them. In this matter of appointments the really decisive action was taken by John XXII. His administrative genius grasped the eventual aim: papal nomination to all benefices, and the necessity to proceed to that aim by stages so as not to excite too much protest. By his constitution *Ex Debito* in 1316 he extended *reservation* to other benefices than those already subject to it, which had hitherto been only those left vacant when their holder died while employed at the papal curia or while at the papal court. A major development was now under way. The austere Benedict XII might aim to eliminate the arbitrary element in the proceedings of John XXII and his subordinates in nominating to major benefices and their excesses in permitting pluralism and *commendation*.[1] He did nothing to alter principles. All his successors followed him: as holy a pope as Urban V considered papal provision as fully justified in law and he extended *reservation* without distinction to patriarchates, archbishoprics, monasteries and nunneries—that is, to *all* major benefices, in 1363. Gregory XI continued his practice. By the second half of the century, then, appointments to all major benefices belonged entirely to the pope and so did appointments to many minor benefices as well. Bishops began to style themselves 'by the grace of God and the Holy See'.

This increased papal power of appointments excited less discontent than might be supposed. The chapters of cathedrals and monasteries were those most likely to protest, but those whom they elected, even before the general reservation of all benefices, were generally quick to have their elections confirmed and so avoid dispute. It may be said that those who held major benefices themselves did much to hasten papal control. It was the same with the holders of minor benefices. A very important category of candidates for these benefices were university scholars and teachers who had no automatic Church appointments and lived mostly from those benefices without cure of souls to which they were appointed; and they found the pope, protector of the universities, much more sympathetic than the average patron and did all they could to get papal reservation extended. Bishops often found it easier and less troublesome to get the pope to nominate their candidates to canonries. Bitter-

[1] Translator's note. A layman, for example, could be 'commended' to hold a benefice and receive its revenues, or men who were not monks could hold office as absentee abbots.

ness came chiefly from lay patrons. Still, popes normally came to understandings with the various kings and rulers on this subject and they usually only nominated candidates whom they had been asked to appoint. The only violent protests came from countries where the papacy's temporal policy favoured a particular party, like the Guelfs in Italy or Lewis of Bavaria's enemies in Germany. Otherwise the complaints came almost wholly from disappointed clergy—though there certainly were some discontented patrons. But altogether it may be said that the clergy favoured the system of papal appointment which seemed to them to ensure greater fairness in the distribution of benefices and whether a better system or not, one which was always more certain and less precarious as a method of being appointed (since there was no appeal against it in law)—in general, therefore, preferable to the old canonical methods of election and patronage.

In this sphere the importance of the centralizing policy of the Avignon popes may be seen: they had established the authority of the pope over the majority of the clergy by making them indebted to the papacy for favours and accustomed to look to Avignon for them. For a clerk named to one benefice would hope for more; even a bishop would hope for translation to a richer and more important bishopric or for extra benefices to hold in plurality. The pope's actions in this matter were felt through the length and breadth of Christendom and thus not only his doctrinal, disciplinary and moral influence was increased, but his political importance also. Clergy given papal benefices struggled against Lewis of Bavaria or the Visconti and helped to create a hostile current of opinion against them, acting as propagandists and sources of news and information.

Doubtless John XXII and his Chamberlain, Gasbert of Laval (who were the principal begetters of all this), would not have done very differently if they had lived in Rome or in some other place than Avignon. But it is at least arguable that Avignon, more centrally placed than Rome, allowed crowds of northern clergy to come as petitioners—and crowds of southern clergy as well. Some of these clergy could probably not have got to Rome. In the same way, being at Avignon helped the pope to extend his authority more easily and rapidly. Administrative centralization of Christendom was inevitable. Avignon made it quicker and more comprehensive.

★   ★   ★

The development of a system of papal taxation was both an aim and a consequence of administrative centralization. Either way the Avignon popes developed it much further.

Papal taxation was originally the result of the crusades. The popes had led them from their origin and it was under the umbrella of taxes to pay for them that papal taxation developed. Until the thirteenth century the pope and cardinals lived from revenues of the papal estates, just as contemporary kings and great lords 'lived of their own'. Innocent III had laid the basis of papal finance: he had got the principle accepted that all benefices should make a contribution to the crusade and he fixed the method by ordering a valuation of benefices and suggesting that they should each contribute a tenth of their net revenues. This was the special crusading tithe—the 'Saladin' tithe.

This idea of a tithe first of all gross and later of all net revenue from benefices was the basis of all later taxation demands. Papal appointment to benefices naturally encouraged the custom that those fortunate enough to be 'provided' to benefices should give as an acknowledgment a present to the pope and to the cardinals who surrounded and advised him and who might be supposed to have assisted in the appointment. The present could be in cash. Gradually these presents were commuted and on a fixed rate proportionate to the benefice concerned—which could be easily ascertained since it was the basis of all other taxation. Taxes on the conferring of benefices grew steadily more numerous and compulsory.

Since the Avignon popes gave themselves such great powers of conferring benefices, taxes on conferment gradually and naturally grew into a system whereby nearly all those appointed to benefices were taxed—after all, from Urban V's time on all holders of major benefices were papally appointed, and so were a great many holders of minor ones.

John XXII had methodically developed the system of papal appointment. He was also the originator of the new taxation and the organizer of Bertrand du Poujet's Italian expedition to establish Bologna as the first base for his return to Rome. The last may seem irrelevant but in fact all three aspects of his policy were closely intertwined: the appointment to benefices enabled the pope to assure himself of the loyalty of the clergy appointed and to raise revenue; the revenue and loyalty meant that a military expedition could be equipped and that it would have diplomatic support and public approval. The papal Chamberlain, Gasbert of Laval (who held the post from 1319 to 1347), was the pope's principal assistant in all this, and was his political and military, as well as his chief financial and administrative, adviser. It may be noted that Benedict XII and Clement VI both continued Gasbert in his post so that he could perfect the papal financial organization.

By the time of Gasbert's death in 1347 the system had been worked out in its entirety. There were five different kinds of revenue which the papacy received:

1. The revenues from *the lands of the Church*, received by the treasurer of the eight provinces of the Papal States and by the Master of the papal mint.

2. The tribute paid in recognition of *papal suzerainty* over various Christian vassal kingdoms (for example, Sicily, or, after King John, England); and the *Census*, paid by monasteries and churches exempt from the authority of their bishops and subject to the pope alone.

3. Taxes on *benefices*, which comprised:

A. '*Services*', that is, taxes paid by all the prelates named, confirmed or translated to their posts by the pope, provided that the revenue of such a bishopric or abbey was worth at least a hundred florins. The sum charged was roughly a third of the annual value of the benefice concerned.

B. '*Visits*', that is, taxes charged on the occasion of the ob-

ligatory '*ad limina*' visits of bishops and abbots 'to the tombs of
the apostles'—that is, to the pope, and, in this period therefore,
to Avignon.

All the above-mentioned revenues were roughly halved between the pope and the cardinals who helped him govern the
Church. All the following taxes on benefices and other sources
of revenue were the pope's solely: they went straight to the
pope's treasury and the cardinal Chamberlain of the sacred
college had nothing to do with them. To continue the taxes on
benefices, then, these were:

C. '*Procurations*', which were sums given by bishops for being
dispensed from residing in or visiting their dioceses.

D. '*Annates*', the first year's revenue of a benefice worth less
than a hundred florins which had been conferred by the pope.

E. '*Spoils*', the pope impounded all goods, movables and
properties of those deceased holders of benefices to whose benefices he reserved the right of reappointment.

F. '*Vacancies*', revenues from vacant benefices kept reserved.

G. '*Charitable subsidies*', forced loans or 'benevolences', 'volun-
tarily' given to the Holy See by benefice holders when it was in
great need.

H. '*Crusading tithes*' or similar taxes—like the tithe for the war
against Lewis of Bavaria in Italy, which the pope defined as a
crusade. Such revenues were often granted away to kings who
had promised to lead a crusade.
4. *The profits of justice* and papal legal jurisdiction.
5. *Gifts, legacies* and various *miscellanea*.
   Roughly half of all papal revenue came from taxes on benefices.
These were then the principal single source, and we have seen
that virtually all taxation on benefices rose from papal appointment to benefices. So administrative centralization and papal
taxation were complementary.
   The principal expenses were:

1. Central administration, the papal court, payment of its officials, the building of the papal palace.
2. War in Italy and the East.
3. The expense of establishments and buildings outside Avignon (for example, St. Peter's) normally at Rome, but elsewhere as well.
4. Charity and alms.

It seems to have been principally Gasbert of Laval who was responsible for working out the organization for collecting revenue, transferring it to Avignon, storing it, making cash payments, controlling expenditure, all under the Camera Apostolica. It seems also that it was he who defined its different departments and functions, established the complicated system of registration, of receipt and expenditure, according to places of origin and destination, and he too who gradually divided Christendom into a certain number of financial areas, each roughly of the same status, and known as 'collectories', since they were the units of collection of papal taxes. Each was either a group of dioceses or a single diocese, sometimes one, sometimes a group of ecclesiastical provinces. Their number was greater in regions where there were more benefices. At the head of each collectory was a collector assisted by auxiliary collectors. The collector received all the revenue and either himself brought it, or saw that it was sent to the Camera Apostolica. Funds were often sent via one of the great commercial companies or Florentine banks with branches at Avignon. The Camera periodically audited each collector's accounts. This financial system did not reach completion till *circa* 1350.

An examination of papal finance in this period leads to two conclusions: that the greater portion of revenue came from the French kingdom (where there were fifteen out of thirty-one collectories) and that the vast majority of expenditure was on the armies which for more than forty years struggled to recover the Papal States. John XXII and Gasbert of Laval organized their financial administration in view of this general principle that funds collected in France would be spent in Italy. The stable residence of the curia at Avignon was strikingly suited for their purposes: Avignon had quite exceptional advantages as a centre for collecting French funds, for controlling them and despatching them to Italy; Avignon was between France and Italy—those were the two countries for relations between which it had most, geographically speaking, to offer.

It is quite certain that the evolution of government and the necessities of the Church would have developed papal finance in the fourteenth century at Rome as they did at Avignon. But it is equally certain that here as elsewhere Avignon's central position in Christendom and its easy access to both France and Italy made things financially easier and more efficient. It is to its residence at Avignon, and to the genius of John XXII and Gasbert of Laval, that the papacy owes the creation of a centralized financial system which has continued to serve it to this day.

★   ★   ★

The financial and administrative centralization of the Church under the authority of the pope favoured a monarchical settlement to those questions of Church government which had been posed by the Gregorian reform.

The pope's authority was expressed throughout Christendom by his legates (to the lessening of the powers of archbishops and metropolitans) and by the obligation of bishops to make an oath of loyalty to the pope and to visit him, which they undertook to do when they were nominated by him. These things gave the pope a direct control of the hierarchy. The increase of reservations and provisions to minor benefices by the pope led to a greater part of the clergy coming to depend on him for their livelihood. The papacy had sheltered the orders of Friars and the universities in their formative period in the thirteenth century and had continually favoured both the Friars and the universities since. Papal provision to benefices was virtually the only form of university pay. All these things ensured that the papacy had the support of the intellectual and spiritual *élite* of Christendom and the clergy, and such support strengthened with the expansion of the system of provisions.

It was, then, with the support of a general consensus of opinion that the papacy continued on general lines of policy mapped out by Gregory VII: the pope issued decretals, underlining that his judgments were the source of canon law; the pope had the sole right to canonize saints; the pope ceaselessly reinforced his powers over bishops, since he alone had the power of translation or of modifying and changing diocesan boundaries; the pope reduced the spiritual powers of bishops by reserving absolution for a whole crowd of sins which were dealt with in his Penitentiary; the pope had the sole right to create *Studia Generalia* (that is, major universities), and in a sense, therefore, he held in his hands the intellectual control of Christendom.

But there was opposition to the papal monarchy from those who preferred less personal methods of government. The cardinals thought of the Holy See as the pope and the sacred college together and thought that they ought to share the pope's authority as they did his revenues. They proposed a more constitutional association of the sacred college in the government of the Church which would have made it more oligarchic and aristocratic, while on the other hand, since Boniface VIII's conflict with Philip the Fair there was a body of opinion which thought that a general council was superior to a pope, and which favoured a semi-parliamentary form of government by successive councils to whom the pope would act as executive. The Avignon popes accentuated monarchy, but they had oligarchy and democracy to contend with.

The cardinals had a considerable part to play in the Church. Since 1059 they, solely, elected the pope. They were his sole counsellors when assembled in Consistory. The pope consulted them on all dogmatic, judicial, territorial matters, on benefices, on the creation of new cardinals; but he alone took the decision. The cardinals were the Holy See's executive officers as legates. They were rich and their small number made them even more influential. To the papal thesis that the pope had full powers and consulted the cardinals only at will, they opposed the notion that the Roman Church was the union of pope and cardinals, as successors of St. Peter and the apostles corporately.

Avignon and the Centralization of the Church

On Clement VI's death in 1352 the cardinals in conclave drew up an agreement by which whoever of them was elected pope would limit the number of cardinals to twenty and would obtain the consent of the cardinals for all important acts of government and for the appointment of new cardinals. Once elected, however, Innocent VI declared the agreement null and void, for the only business a conclave could transact was the election of a pope, and it could do no other; he continued to refuse to allow the sacred college to meet save at his orders and he kept it in order by new creations.

The cardinals had failed and the two returns of the pope to Rome, despite the plainly expressed opposition of the majority of the cardinals, showed the strength of the pope's authority. But once the pope was dead the cardinals governed the Church during the interregnum and it was then that they showed their power. It was the cardinals who made the schism of 1378. That schism is the proof of their power, however much successive popes disciplined them. Just as they started the schism, though, so they tried to end it. The cardinals of both obediences broke their allegiances in 1408 and called the council of Pisa. If their suggestions had taken effect, if both popes had resigned, if the pope chosen by the cardinals, Alexander V, had become the sole lawful pope,[1] then the power of the sacred college in the Church would have been greatly reinforced and an oligarchy might have been established. But the flat refusal of the popes at Avignon and Rome to resign made Alexander V's election useless and only added a third contender, discredited the cardinals and reinforced the principle of papal monarchy in the two obediences.

The conciliar movement did not die with Boniface VIII. The custom of summoning councils to deal with the principal questions under discussion in the Church was strong enough for a weak pope, Clement V, to summon the council of Vienne, in order to examine with the prelates and doctors of Christendom

[1] Translator's note. As his numbering shows, normal practice has included Alexander V among the lawful popes, but it has equally recognised the pope who continued to rule the Roman obedience, Gregory XII. For a list of popes and antipopes see the appendix.

the constant problem of the reform of the Church, the crusade and the tiresome but very serious business of the fate of the Templars. But the council of Vienne was called by the pope: it was the pope who drew up the agenda and chaired the debates, which he interrupted at will for negotiations with the king of France; and it was the pope who imposed the solutions —in particular the dissolution of the Templars, to which the majority of the council was hostile. The pope had, then, behaved as sole and absolute head of the Church in the context of a council which had some pretensions to direct the Church itself.

Despite this precedent the pope's enemies continued to call for a council. Philip the Fair had shown how to do it; only a council could re-establish normal life in a Church saddled with a heretic pope. Consequently, it was sufficient to accuse a pope of heresy, as Philip had accused Boniface, to justify the calling of a council, and it could then be maintained that such a council's decisions could overrule a pope. John XXII's rash propositions on the subject of the Beatific Vision gave an ideal handle to his enemies, particularly to Lewis of Bavaria, who had been demanding a council since 1323.

For many reasons, therefore, a council seemed dangerous to Clement V's successors; they never called one—and that fact alone attests their power over the Church and their increasing absolutism. It required the appalling troubles of the schism for conciliarism to revive and for a council to seem the sole way out. Public opinion then demanded one so strongly that one had to be called. We have seen what happened to the council of Pisa (1409), the cardinals' council. It failed. It was the council of Constance (1414–18), called by the German emperor, which was successful in resolving the schism. The council fathers laid down that to escape similar scandals the Church should be governed by similar councils, to be summoned every ten years. But the fifteenth-century popes were able to prevent this proposal coming to anything. Eugenius IV crushed the council of Basel (1431–49) and restored the papal monarchy. The conciliar movement failed because the Avignon popes had established the papal monarchy too strongly and because the tendency of political thought in the West, above all in France, was towards absolutism, and because, despite some misgivings in some breasts, absolutism was to prevail.

Both the demands for the rights of the sacred college and the various affirmations of conciliar teaching reflect, in the context of the Church's government, the constitutional debates in contemporary Western kingdoms. To kings who wanted to exercise the absolutism which the Roman law gave them were opposed the partisans of the rights of a king's feudal vassals to counsel him in government, and a wider general movement of noble, clerical and urban opinion which wanted to give a greater place in government to privileged bodies organized in assemblies—assemblies of 'Estates'. In the course of a struggle which still continued in the early fifteenth century, the kings of France in particular had extended their power: by eliminating their great vassals, accepting a direct feudal relation through homage with a larger and larger number of lesser men (who had previously been subinfeoffed to those great vassals); by multiplying officials; by summoning more and more appeals to their court; by making more and more cases *royal* cases; and by obtaining, through the creation of a taxation system justified by war, the financial means for conducting a policy which they could never have followed on the basis of the revenues they obtained from their own lands.

This parallel between the increase of papal power and royal power applies quite closely if we take the kingdom of France as the model. The set-backs which both the papacy and the French kingdom met in their development of absolutism were similar, even if they were not synonymous, and both pope and king finally triumphed in the mid-fifteenth century. But while the Holy See's residence at Avignon undoubtedly favoured the development of the centralization of the Church administratively and financially, it is by no means as clear that it so affected the development of the constitutional centralization of the Church and the growth of the papal monarchy. If there were borrowings from the French kingdom by the Church, or *vice versa*, they were mutual borrowings. Just the same, it ought not to be forgotten that it was in the French kingdom that royal absolutism developed most successfully, that France was in close touch with Avignon and that the Avignon popes of the period before the schism had all of them grown up, and two of them personally served, in the French kingdom; and also that they were the popes who put the papal power in a condition to weather the appalling fifty-year crisis of a divided Christendom.

VII

Papal Patronage at Avignon

The stable residence of the popes at Avignon, and the increase in their revenues, gave them both an occasion and an opportunity to favour arts and letters on a scale quite beyond the reach of their predecessors.

At Avignon the building of two successive palaces, the uninterrupted stay of the popes there, and the abundance of their funds, all created a real efflorescence of patronage. Before the schism the Avignon popes devoted on the average about 4 per cent of their revenue to purely intellectual and artistic purposes. The cardinals did likewise. Naturally, patronage was particularly generous under certain open-handed popes like Clement VI, Gregory XI and 'Clement VII', and certain cardinals in particular were remarkable for their encouragement of art and learning, but these examples created imitation, a way of life and a habit of mind.

The construction and decoration of the palace itself meant an entire artistic programme. If among architects both Benedict XII and Clement VI selected mediocre local men, Pierre Poisson and John of Loubières, they got their decorators from far and wide. The tomb of John XXII in the cathedral seems to have been largely the work of an English sculptor. For the decoration of the vast areas of wall space inside the palace, with its relatively few windows, the popes had the alternatives of the northern solution—tapestry: or the southern solution—fresco. They chose, as southerners (and the choice shows how southern they were), fresco; and the Italians were the masters of fresco.

Cardinal Stefaneschi seems to have been the patron who brought to Avignon one of the best living Italian painters and the one who, because of his Gothic tendencies, was most likely to be appreciated in a northern milieu. This was Simone Martini of Siena. He arrived in Avignon in 1339. Benedict XII was Cistercian enough not to want interior decoration in his palace-monastery. Martini found his great opportunity then in decorating the walls of churches. In the tympanum of the portal of the cathedral he painted one of his masterpieces—Our Lady giving suck to the Child—which became the prototype of thousands of paintings of Our Lady of Humility in Italy, France Germany and Spain in the fourteenth and fifteenth centuries. He had created a new iconographical theme. Martini died at Avignon in 1344. Many of his relations and pupils had followed him, his brother-in-law, Lippo Memmi, for one. The most remarkable was Matteo Giovanelli of Viterbo to whom Clement VI gave the task of decorating the chapels of St. Martial and St. John Baptist and many other rooms in the new palace. In those rooms what Clement VI wanted was essentially the feel of those northern tapestries which had surrounded him at Fécamp, Sens, Rouen and Paris. It was essentially themes for tapestry which were painted on these walls, foliage, hunting and fishing. Some of the decoration still survives in the famous Room of the Stag, and for that room it seems that a group of Frenchmen from northern France and a group of Burgundians and men from the Rhône collaborated with Giovanelli's men.

Similar but less ambitious schemes of painting were commissioned by the popes in the castles and abbeys which they built round Avignon and by the cardinals in their palaces, villas and religious foundations. Thus, before the palace at Avignon was built, John XXII built the palace at Sorgues and the castle at Châteauneuf-Calcernier, and Innocent VI built the Charterhouse at Villeneuve. Among the foundations made by cardinals the most important is the collegiate church of Villeneuve, founded by the Cardinal Arnaud de Via.

Inside the painted rooms of the papal palace there were the collections of *objets d'art*, and in its gardens, the collections of plants and animals. The papal collections were partly the result of gifts, but the popes also bought extensively, above all, jewels, metalwork, goldsmiths' work and the sacred vessels of gold and silver which the papal treasury would melt down or pawn in its fits of bankruptcy. But as in all contemporary royal and princely collections there was a strange clutter of objects—anything provided that it was exotic or odd. This taste for curiosities expressed itself in the papal zoo with its bears, a camel, stags and many other animals.

One of these collections has special interest—the collection of manuscripts, which gradually grew into a library. John XXII and Benedict XII began mainly with liturgical manuscripts and theological and legal manuscripts for a working reference library, books indispensable for Church government, Church ceremonies and the pope's own devotions. But from Clement VI's time on there was a new kind of book (and the tendency continued under Urban V): books on the crusade—always of major and constant interest—Hebrew books, translations from the Arabic, and, above all, Latin classical literature. These books reveal intellectual interests—there were no professional reasons for acquiring them; they reveal as well the influence of Petrarch and the humanists. The papal secretaries who wrote the pope's letters used the pope's money to buy the great classical texts which they could use as models of thought and style. The choice of such secretaries was in itself a new sort of patronage.

Patronage of humanists continued under Gregory XI who gave a salary to a Greek philosopher, and humanists were particularly favoured by 'Clement VII' and by 'Benedict XIII'. The catalogues of the papal library which survive from their time contain works of history, general chronicles, Latin literature and all the Latin works of Petrarch. On the eve of 'Benedict XIII's' departure for Peñiscola, to which he carried off one thousand and ninety manuscripts, the papal library had at least one thousand five hundred, if not two thousand books.

The cardinals each had a library, composed on much the same lines, usually, as the papal library. The best contained, according to their catalogues, about a hundred and fifty to two hundred manuscripts. These libraries were used by their secretaries and they and the papal secretaries boasted of their Latin style, corresponding with Italian humanists like Coluccio Salutati, the humanist secretary of the Florentine republic. Between them they made Avignon one of the principal centres of Western humanism.

The popes showed their taste for patronage in the way they recruited and developed their chapel. The papal chapel could be expected to be musically well served but its great numbers and the way in which singers and musicians were recruited from northern lands (especially from Liège, long the most famous musical centre of Christendom), alike show a real musical enthusiasm and funds available to satisfy it.

The popes commissioned splendid works of art, but quite apart from the great interest of these in themselves, this papal patronage has a particular interest in that it assembled artists from all over Christendom and thus made contact between widely different cultural areas and allowed them to influence each other. The popes made Avignon a cultural meeting-point and an important centre of cultural transmission.

It is only necessary to think of the influence of Simone Martini and the Sienese painters on French art, which by the end of the fourteenth century adopted the style which we call inter-national Gothic; of the diffusion of copies of 'Our Lady of Humility'; of the influence of the Catalan and Aragonese painters (summoned by 'Benedict XIII') on Provençal paint-ing; of the knowledge of Petrarch and Boccaccio diffused among northern writers who translated (at Avignon) their works into French, and not only their Latin works but, like the translator Laurent of Premierfait, their Italian ones; and of the imitation by the Aragonese court of Franco-Flemish polyphony brought to the papal chapel by musicians from Liège. In this role Avignon was greatly helped by the establishment at Aix-en-Provence of the court of 'Sicily' whose members had constant contact with Angers, Paris and Naples.

What is striking is that even after the popes left (though a temporary return continued to be hoped for) Avignon remained a more important intellectual and artistic centre than Aix. Its university kept its prestige despite the creation of the university at Aix at the beginning of the fifteenth century, and artists from different countries, Flanders, France, Burgundy and Italy, continued to come there to work. The masterpiece of this artistic centre which the popes created and the legates kept alive is the Pietà of Villeneuve-les-Avignon which is full of the Gothic spirit and in which Catalan influence can be clearly perceived. If one reflects that the master of the Aix Annunciation knew Van Eyck and transmitted his thought and aesthetics from Aix to Avignon, to the master of Antonello of Messina—that is, to the Italians—then it can be said that Avignon's central position was as important intellectually and artistically as it was financially and administratively, and that papal patronage made it a place of contact between the great arts of the north and the south.

VIII

The Avignon Popes and
the Spiritual Life of the Church

Sedentariness and centralization, then, had developed papal
taxation and papal patronage at Avignon. The Church
became a monarchy, exceptional in its international nature
but in some ways very like other contemporary national monarchies which developed much the same characteristics.

This papal monarchy had evolved progressively; Gregory VII
had revived ideas expressed in much older texts and the whole
development was greatly accelerated when the popes took on
the direction of the crusades, and when, initially, the crusades
were successful. It was to re-establish the hapless Christian
states of the East and to reconquer the Holy Land that the
thirteenth-century popes had taken control of the Church and
begun to tax it in a way which affected every holder of a benefice. The Avignon popes had the same over-riding interest. A
victorious crusade was the ultimate aim of all their policy, it
was what justified the establishment of papal monarchy; and
the reconquest of the Italian lands of the papacy and the re-
establishment of French-English harmony were only necessary
preliminaries to a crusade. But sheer force of circumstance
compelled the popes to spend more and more time on the preliminaries. At the very moment at which the Church became a
centralized monarchy, the very aim of that organization, the
reconquest and protection of the Christian East, seemed neglected and even abandoned. The century began with the dissolution of the Templars, who were the living symbols as an order
of the whole crusading era and who became the scapegoats of

an ashamed and disgraced Christendom. It went on to see the retreat of the Hospitallers to Rhodes, the disappearance of all independent Christian states in Syria and Palestine and the Turkish threat to Constantinople. The popes for all their good intentions and efforts could do nothing about it. The centralized and monarchic government of the Church found no justification then in that successful crusade which was its excuse and cause.

Nor did the Church undergo the moral reform which had been Gregory VII's impulse and ambition. Since the twelfth century no grand general effort for reform had been undertaken.[1] After 1311 the popes called no council and therefore made themselves responsible for the relaxation of the moral and spiritual life of the Church.

Certain contemporaries were peculiarly conscious of this moral decline and thought that it was the fault of the papacy. They used the failure of the crusades, for which, in a general and slightly muddled fashion the papacy was held responsible, to criticize its centralizing policy strongly and vigorously. The pope's residence at Avignon far from the tombs of the apostles, the luxurious palace with its treasury lodged in its strongest tower, the complicated administration, the numerous court, all seemed symptomatic of irredeemable worldliness. What was the Vicar of Christ doing raising taxes, equipping armies, reconquering lands? Was he any different from any other king? His spiritual office seemed obscured by his temporal concerns and his example justified every sort of abuse. It was not only enemies who said so. Guillaume Durand, the bishop of Mende, and Alvaro Pelayo, the Austin Friar, had no axes to grind, and they speak of numerous abuses, which were, in fact, the by-product of centralization. The popes from the Langue d'Oc had gone back to the old Roman nepotism. It might be human to have family affections and local ties, it might be natural that the popes should surround themselves with people they could

---

[1] Translator's note. Professor Renouard is perhaps over hard on the thirteenth-century councils, particularly the Lateran council of 1215, thirteenth-century legislation, and the Friars.

trust; still, how was it that the papal court was Gascon under Clement V, from Quercy under John XXII and from the Limousin under Clement VI and his successors? The grant of expectative benefices often gave rise to the appointment of extremely unsuitable candidates. The cardinals, the curia, the principal prelates and the teachers at the universities all lived by pluralism and absenteeism: how could they behave like this to cures of souls? The faithful must be neglected unless their pastors and masters were to acquire the habit of bilocation or ubiquity. The multiplication of taxes and crusading tithes which bore so heavily on the clergy and faithful might be excused if they served to equip expeditions for the Holy Land, but most of these revenues were either passed on by the popes to kings who used them selfishly, or were spent by the popes themselves in Italian wars. Finally, the corruption of those curial officials who shamelessly exploited and milked petitioners for benefices made an easy target for enemies of centralization and papal monarchy.

These critics tended to be either Franciscans or laymen.

Since St. Francis's time his disciples had tried to organize a common life based above all on poverty. However, a common life in itself and the need (for instance) to train preachers seemed to some, the 'Conventuals', to require a mitigation of poverty which their opponents, the 'Spirituals', who were nearer to the order's primitive and eremitical origins,[1] believed could only be absolute.

John XXII, following Boniface VIII, entered this debate in 1322–3 by first refusing to 'hold' the property of the Franciscans for them—a fiction which had been adopted since Nicholas III's time—and then condemning the doctrine that Christ and the apostles possessed nothing either of their own or in common. Willy-nilly, the Franciscans were now property owners. John XXII's position was the logical position for an administrator who intended to preserve the unity of the order, the common-

---

[1] Translator's note. This whole question is highly controversial. For an excellent treatment, see M. D. Lambert, *Franciscan Poverty* (London, S.P.C.K., 1961).

sense position of a practical man without mystical tendencies who regarded absolute poverty as an intellectual chimera, the position of a monarchically-minded pope who was not going to admit that the Rule of St. Francis was outside papal control and who denied the 'Spirituals' ' view that absolute poverty was a gospel precept. His decision alienated not only the 'Spirituals' but also some 'Conventuals'. They accused him of heresy for his interpretation of the Rule of St. Francis, and his theories on the Beatific Vision gave colour to the accusation. The most advanced, the 'Fraticelli', shut out from the Church by the pope's decision, proclaimed that they constituted the true Church, the Gospel Church renewed by St. Francis, persecuted by the false Church, that of the popes.

In their anarchical criticism of the hierarchy, of monarchy and dogmatism, the 'Spirituals' and other Franciscans found lay support. Their most eminent supporter was Marsiglio of Padua. Marsiglio, basing himself on the Gospel and on the organization of the primitive Church, denied the pope all rights to plentitude of power and affirmed the right of the laity to intervene in that Church of which they were a part, quite as much as the clergy, to repress the scandals of the papal monarchy. These ideas were taken up by the English Franciscan, William of Ockham, and then, in the last quarter of the fourteenth century, by the English university teacher and writer, John Wycliffe, and by a group of Czech thinkers.

These spontaneous and simultaneous criticisms from Franciscans and laymen, lawyers and politicians, drew their strength from deep currents of thought both popular and intellectual. Contrasted with the ostentatious wealth of the merchants and princes enriched by trade and new taxation, the poverty extolled by the Franciscans appeared as the true test for salvation in a world where Dives and his followers were damned in Hell. It was a widespread belief and a comforting one, which spread among the humble and pricked at the consciences of the powerful, and its importance is manifest in the large size of the Franciscan Third Order and in the voluntary poverty movements of laymen under Franciscan influence. It was reinforced by a belief in the approaching end of the world which became active in response to the many disasters of the fourteenth century, the wars, the Black Death of 1348–51, with its later recurrences, bad harvests, famines. One aspect was a deep mysticism with a morbid extreme fringe like the Flagellants, but itself a genuine form of the religious life where what was sought was deeper knowledge of God. The means were the multiplication of devotions, the cult of the saints who interceded between God and man, and intense prayer.

This widely-spread movement among the laity was developed by preaching and by the example of the Friars who lived in the towns and created 'third orders' for the laity to join. It was given inspiration by the life of Christ and his apostles in the Gospels, and Simone Fidate of Cascia and Ludolf the Carthusian both wrote the first Lives of Jesus, with an emphasis on our Lord's humanity and His everyday life. In countries like Germany, which long lay under interdict during the papal struggle with Lewis of Bavaria, the absence of all liturgical ceremonies helped to develop prayer in common and the mystical life of the laity. In the Rhine valley and the Low Countries under the influence of the friaries there arose and flourished the 'Béguinage' movement whose devotional life was nourished by the works of Tauler, Eckhart, Suso and Ruysbroeck. Many of the nobility and middle class, men and women, could read and their piety was sustained by devotional reading as well as by preaching. The women read the Hours of Our Lady; and all had available to them the New Testament, the epistles of St. Paul in the vernacular, and the treatises of Ruysbroeck (which were written in Flemish but translated, like those of Suso and Eckhart, into all the German dialects). The Dominican order was declining in numbers, partly because of the Black Death, and did not have the forces at its disposal to direct these new developments.

Such a society in which increased prosperity, literacy and elementary education alike increased a more personal and devotional religion in the towns—such a society tended to be shocked and alienated from both papacy and bishops by their worldliness and by the collapse of any common Christian policy in face of the national divisions which now rent Christendom. Many thought of the Black Death as a Judgment. There was no sort of communication or agreement between this sort of lay opinion and the Avignon popes. Since Celestine V had resigned the papacy the popes had not been mystics. With the exception of Benedict XII, they had not even been theologians. The Avignon popes were lawyers: nearly all of them had taught law and undertaken ecclesiastical administration. Most of their cardinals were canon lawyers. They showed a strong tendency to organize the Church as a vast administrative machine and to think of the Christian life as a matter of juridical relationships rather than as a real and living relationship between God and man. They thought in terms of dogma, imposed by laws and decretals, controlled by an Inquisition which stamped out heresy mercilessly: breaches of the law brought penalties—those of the Inquisition for heresy, those of the papal Penitentiary for lesser sins. A system of indulgences could mitigate such penalties.

The Avignon popes were building a strong, centralized, monarchical Church. They scarcely saw the deeper tendencies of contemporary Christian thinking, and would have been out of sympathy if they had. They were absorbed in their great, ceaseless, appallingly difficult temporal tasks of the reconquest of the Holy Land and the reunion of the churches and they did not have the qualities to appeal to a disquieted and worried Christendom. None of them tried to raise and rouse the Church by a great and far-reaching reformation. They were steady religious men, but they were not apostles; there was nothing to fire and inspire the Church, nothing to turn it from an administrative hierarchy to something living. Benedict XII was an austere man but his reforms were only in details. To sum up, the Avignon popes failed to make a full contact with an increasingly eductated Christian opinion, or with the strong otherworldliness of contemporary mysticism. Only a council, men might think, could bring about the great necessary reform and restore a Church of the Gospel.

None the less, in the fourteenth century the pope's authority over all Christendom was both maintained and expanded. Both the hierarchy of bishops and abbots who were papally nominated to their positions, and the whole body of clergy who hoped to be provided to benefices, were deeply and wholly attached to them; and their influence deepened the natural feelings of the faithful for the Holy Father. Neither the general latent anti-clericalism nor the impulse of the new mysticism was sufficient to bring about the calling of a general council, and the fact that one was not even demanded before 1380 shows how powerful the papacy had become. The general respect for the frequent and prolonged interdicts which the popes laid on kings shows how normal and natural obedience to them was. The immense success of the Jubilee of 1350 shows their authority and prestige in a different way. The development of indulgences was not only financially profitable, it also chimed with popular feeling and gave men a chance they wished for—to escape temporal as well as eternal penance. Here at least the popes were in touch with popular religion.

The very tendencies which were to bring about the Reformation were obscure and difficult to perceive, but they were there and developed while the whole problem of Reform was left unsolved. By the time a council had been called to end the schism public opinion had lost faith in the papacy's power and wish to reform, scandalized as it was by the involvement of the Church with temporal affairs and still further by the schism. It was generally thought that only a general council could bring about that reform in head and members which the Avignon popes had made even more necessary by concentrating so much power in their own hands.

IX

The Avignon Popes and the Christian World

Since the Gregorian reform the popes had not only claimed a more and more direct authority over the Church, but also a supreme headship of Christian society.

First of all, as holder of the power of binding and loosing conferred by our Lord on St. Peter, the pope could call any Christian before his judgment *ratione peccati*, because of his sins. Neither kings nor the Emperor himself were exempt from this jurisdiction, the pope's *magisterium* over the faithful, and Gregory VII, for moral and spiritual reasons, had used it to depose the Emperor Henry IV.[1] To this moral basis for papal supremacy there had been added another in political theory, based on the text in the gospels which speaks of 'two swords'.[2] Papal partisans interpreted it as a quite clear declaration of the pope's general supremacy. 'One sword must submit to the other, temporal authority must be below spiritual', said Boniface VIII in his bull *Unam Sanctam*. This unitary notion of Christendom, indeed of the world itself, as entirely and absolutely under the pope's authority as its spiritual head and the Vicar of Christ had been reinforced by the essential monism of Thomist philosophy, which triumphed in the thirteenth-century universities which received their charters and support from the pope. John XXII canonized St. Thomas, and it shows in what esteem the fourteenth-century popes held him and his system. Practical ex-

[1] Translator's note. For a recent review of Gregory's actions in this *cause célèbre*, see K. F. Morrison, 'Canossa, a revision', *Traditio*, vol. 18, 1962, pp. 121–48.

[2] Translator's note. Luke xxii. 38: 'See, Lord, they told him, here are two swords and he answered, That is enough.'

amples of the pope's sovereignty over the world are the concessions of discoveries in the New and Old worlds to the sovereigns of the discoverers (the kings of Castile and Portugal) and the papal coronation of the Holy Roman Emperors from 800 onwards (when the pope crowned Charlemagne). Papal sovereignty was reinforced by the whole system of feudal submission of vassal kingdoms to the Holy See, which was further developed by Innocent III in an attempt to build up Christendom into a sort of feudal pyramid with the pope at its head and the various kings bound to him by personal oaths of loyalty.

Philip the Fair brutally called the whole system in question when he attacked Boniface VIII (who had proclaimed papal rights rising from this system so tactlessly and inopportunely) in person at Anagni. The king of France had vindicated the temporal authority of the princes of Europe; he had claimed to speak in the name of the faith itself when he accused Boniface of heresy—in taking the papacy from a predecessor who was alive when he took it; he had been supported by French public opinion, ready to believe in his piety as St. Louis's grandson; he had taken the measure of that public opinion in unprecedentedly representative assemblies.

Benedict XI was cautious enough to avoid the issue by pretending that Philip had not instigated the outrage, and only condemned his accomplices. The theoretical problem remained, however. Philip put pressure on Clement V by threatening him with a council to condemn Boniface posthumously. It seems likely that he had come to some agreement with the papacy when Clement was elected. Clement did not abandon any theocratic principles, but he did, on February 3rd, 1306, quite plainly and simply revoke the two bulls *Unam Sanctam* and *Clericis Laicos* in which Boniface had flatly applied his theocratic powers against Philip. The revocation was a serious step and a serious reverse. There was more to come: Philip blackmailed Clement with the threat of reviving his attacks on Boniface; he forced him to suppress the Templars at the council of Vienne and by so doing showed that the roles had changed and that the temporal power could control the spiritual. Clement V did maintain papal supremacy over the Empire against the German Emperor, Henry VII, he refused to come to Rome to crown him and he supported Robert of Naples against him; but he only spoke of the rights over the Empire which he derived from his *plenitudo potestatis* after Henry VII's death. The principles might have been safeguarded, but the pope's double collapse before the king of France and the Emperor showed that any real assertion of the pope's sovereignty over the world was beyond hope. The whole idea was in irremediable decline.

There were two claimants to Henry's succession, Lewis of Bavaria and Frederick of Austria, both of whom were crowned as 'King of the Romans' in 1314. John XXII decided to reap the advantages of their rivalry both for papal claims to sovereignty over the Empire in general and his Italian policy in particular, since neither of the rival princes, as long as they were rivals, would be able to interfere with his reconquest there. He stated that until a papal decision had been made no candidate for the Empire could be 'King of the Romans', but only King-elect. It was therefore in effect for the pope to choose the 'King of the Romans'. In that situation he declared that he was unable to judge as to which candidate had been properly elected since he had received no official notification of either election. As officially, therefore, there had been no election, the position of 'King of the Romans' was vacant. Since, moreover, when the Empire was vacant it was for the pope to administer it (according to a decretal of Clement V's), John XXII assumed the imperial powers in Italy and named his vassal Robert of Naples as imperial vicar there.

John XXII's Italian policy, in fact, very largely determined his stand on principle. After Lewis of Bavaria's victory at Mühldorf John XXII preserved the advantages of his position by refusing to recognize Lewis as even a candidate for the Empire, since his election had not been authorized by the papacy. Lewis of Bavaria replied by proclaiming at Frankfurt on Main in 1324 that the decision was not the pope's at all, but that it was the imperial electors who ended an interregnum: it was from them that a 'King of the Romans' held his power, and even the imperial coronation by the pope conferred no fresh rights. Having taken up their respective extreme and opposite positions the two adversaries proceeded to fight it out with a violence worthy of Gregory VII and Henry IV themselves. The resemblance to the Investiture Contest, however, was merely superficial. There was very little public reaction to it all.

John XXII excommunicated Lewis. Lewis took his support from the old imperial tradition of Caesaropapism, from what had been said by Philip the Fair's lawyers, from the doctrines supplied to him by Marsiglio of Padua, John of Jandun and William of Ockham. The teaching of Marsiglio and John of Jandun was expressed in the *Defensor Pacis* of 1324, a treatise which maintained the supremacy of *civil* power alike over temporal and spiritual. This teaching combined well with that of Ockham who believed in a totally separated Church and State. Ockham was a Franciscan and had behind him the 'Spiritual' party among the Franciscans who were in revolt against the pope. Lewis had, of course, the political support of the Italian Ghibellines. In the consciousness of all this support Lewis accused John of heresy and at Sachsenhausen in 1324 summoned him before a General Council. Then he marched into Italy, had himself proclaimed Emperor by the Roman people (this was the way that Marsiglio said that a Roman Emperor should be made) and had himself crowned in St. Peter's in 1328. John XXII replied by calling Lewis a heretic, relieving his vassals of any obligation to him and preaching a crusade against him. Naturally Lewis replied that he was no heretic, but that John was, because he denied Gospel teaching on imperial sovereignty in temporal matters and because he dared to release imperial subjects of their sworn oaths: he, as Emperor, had a God-given power against malefactors, and, using it, he deposed John and chose a new pope, the 'Spiritual' Franciscan, Peter of Corbara, who took the name 'Nicholas V'. Such a direct deposition of a pope by an Emperor had no precedent later than Henry IV's time in the late eleventh century and it highlights the violence, anachronism and complexity of the quarrel. But when the Guelfs took the field Lewis had to leave alike Rome and Italy, and the deserted 'Nicholas' submitted to John XXII in 1330.

Neither side spared extreme measures or violent abuse, but it all came to nothing. The paradox is that the one wanted to establish his authority in Italy and the other his authority in Germany. They could easily have divided spheres of influence. However, once John XXII had enunciated his principles (called forth as they were by his Italian policy), the fight was on. Public opinion thought of Lewis as lawful Emperor and John as lawful pope, but they continued to struggle ideologically and pointlessly.

Benedict XII and Clement VI took the same line as John XXII: the high theocratic line, that only the papal recognition makes a candidate elected by the electors more than a King-*elect* of the Romans. Lewis refused to acknowledge that he was less than 'King of the Romans' and demanded that the pope should recognize that he was. The electors, in the Declaration of Rhens in 1338, backed Lewis, who, after all, was glorifying them in making them the sole source of his royal power, and the qualifying source of imperial power, since an Emperor must first be elected 'King of the Romans'.

The struggle died down, though. Public opinion was disturbed by the interdict which John XXII had laid on Germany; Lewis's family policy of dynastic aggrandisement disquieted the electors. In order to have peace they accepted Clement VI's suggestion that they should elect another 'King of the Romans', and they elected Charles of Moravia, Henry VII's grandson, who gave the pope all the assurances he could wish for with regard to the papal lands in Italy. Clement recognized Charles as 'King of the Romans' in 1346. The papacy and theocratic doctrine seemed to have had the last word.

But once Charles was crowned Emperor (after a hasty trip to Italy in 1355), he laid down the norms and procedures for electing a 'King of the Romans' in the Golden Bull of 1356 where he never mentioned anything at all about papal confirmation of the election in a text which was henceforth to be regarded as basic; and Innocent VI did not protest because he needed Charles's support against the Visconti. For this same reason when, in 1359–60, Innocent VI at Charles IV's request declared that Clement V had not intended to disparage the memory of Charles's grandfather, Henry VII, in those bulls which Clement had issued after Henry's death declaring that the spiritual power was superior to the temporal, Innocent said nothing about that superiority. His silence may be taken as a tacit abandonment of the position. To crown it all, Charles had his son, Wenceslas (the Fool), elected and crowned 'King of the Romans' in 1376 without bothering to obtain a papal confirmation of the election. Charles had appeared to accept theocratic teachings about papal supremacy over the 'King of the Romans' and the Emperor when he was trying to obtain the Empire; now he was Emperor he did not bother about them. The old principles were left undisturbed and undiscussed. As far as territorial claims went for the pope in Italy and the Emperor in Germany the old ideology was tacitly abandoned and the notion that Church and Empire were separate came to be generally accepted both by the princes and the public at large. In a nutshell, from 1350 on, papal supremacy over the Empire was an idea with no practical consequences.

It was the same with the whole idea, developed by Innocent III, of papal suzerainty over Christendom created by oaths of feudal loyalty taken by vassal kings to the Holy See. The visible sign of this suzerainty was an annual tribute. During the fourteenth century the majority of the vassal kings stopped paying, showing that they no longer recognized their obligation.

The clearest case was England. Edward III stopped paying his annual tribute in 1333. Papal suzerainty was not abolished, but it was never mentioned, and the symbolic payment stopped. A tactless demand of Urban V's in 1366 for thirty-three years of arrears led to a strong reaction. Edward III consulted clergy, lords and commons, and they relieved him of his obligation, because King John's donation of the country to the Holy See in 1213 had been made without counsel or consent and was against his coronation oath. Papal suzerainty over England was thus abruptly abolished. Its abolition was part of a series of anti-papal moves. Since the beginning of the century Parliament had protested against papal provision of absentees to English benefices; against papal taxation for the French king's benefit, to turn English money into French weapons directed against England; and against the calling of cases relating to benefices to Avignon. The Statutes of Provisors (1351) and of Praemunire (1353) had underlined Parliament's feelings and made it clear that the English Church's allegiance to the pope was purely spiritual. After the Treaty of Brétigny, which crowned the victories God had given him, Edward III had gained his full sovereignty over Aquitaine and no longer wanted or asked papal help, and proudly rejected any claims of suzerainty. Public opinion supported him.

Papal suzerainty only went on being exercised over weak kings who wanted the pope's help. That was the situation of the French kings of 'Sicily' who had been invested with Sicily by the pope in 1265, driven out of the island by the Aragonese after the 'Sicilian Vespers' in 1282, and needed papal help to re-establish themselves in the lost half of their kingdom. This limitation of the papal suzerainty made the pope into the head of an alliance or party rather than a universal overlord. The pope's vassal, the king of 'Sicily' was head of the Guelf alliance in Italy, owned Avignon till 1348, and was the pope's protector there in his capacity as count of Provence. It was he who dealt with the Emperor when he descended on Rome for his coronation. He was supported by the Florentine merchant companies who had aided the triumph of the French cause in south Italy and who had ruthlessly despoiled the south Italian kingdom, as well as being the pope's bankers throughout Christendom. In the East, in Sicily, in Majorca, the popes opposed the Aragonese because they were the enemies of the French 'Sicilian' kings, building up a Mediterranean empire at their expense. The 'Sicilian' princes of the House of Anjou were the cousins of the French Valois, and the French popes, living at Avignon, on the edge of France, constantly gave the Valois kings diplomatic and financial help against the English kings in their great dynastic struggle which so continually frustrated any new crusade.

Thus, throughout the fourteenth century the pope's general sovereignty of the world was maintained and sometimes spectacularly affirmed: it was in the right of it that the popes granted newly-discovered lands to the first Christian discoverers, like the Fortunate Islands (the Canaries) which Clement VI gave in fief to Luis de la Cerda in 1344, and it was in right of it that they played their diplomatic role as peacemakers and tried to heal all the quarrels they could between Christian princes and lords. But in practice they were careful not to invoke their *dominium mundi* against either the Emperor or the powerful kings of France or England.

★   ★   ★

The cause of this general relaxation of papal authority over Christian princes was a general evolution of new political theory in the fourteenth century. The development of the Roman law taught in the faculties of civil law to lawyers who subsequently became royal counsellors led them to urge its principles of absolute power on their masters. Dualist Ockhamist philosophy in Oxford, Paris, Germany and Italy gave the theological justification to this revival of classical theories: like Faith and Reason, State and Church should be wholly separated and not interfere in each other's separate spheres; neither the Emperor nor kings then should be said to hold their powers from the pope.

Kings making themselves absolute had to have religious justification. They found it in their coronation services—particularly the kings of France who were anointed with a miraculous oil brought from heaven to St. Remigius at the baptism of King Clovis. The king derived his power direct from God, as was plain from the power he had, immediately after his coronation, of healing a skin disease, the scrofula (or King's Evil) by miraculous touch. It did not come from the pope. This Divine Right with its mystical element undoubtedly assisted royal rule.

Though kingdoms in the fourteenth century appeared and evolved in different ways, they were similar in that they were political units closely grouped round their king with a centralized administration, a taxation system which tended to create regular annual taxes and a strong public sentiment felt for a king who claimed divine right for his rule. These political units tended to become exclusive and xenophobic, shut off from each other and fighting among themselves. There was a growth of national self-consciousness which went with a growth of national vernacular literatures. It was more and more difficult for the popes to be international sovereigns over these national unities, each self-sufficient, each with its own public opinion. This was shown in the way that the Church of France supported Philip the Fair, or in which the annual convocations of the clergy supported Edward III in his resistance to papal demands. At the time when inside the various kingdoms lay jurisdiction was whittling away ecclesiastical jurisdiction there was no hope of sustaining an international papal sovereignty. The close ties of the Avignon popes to France made them suspect moreover in other countries, especially England and Italy.

The schism which broke out in 1378 weakened this already declining authority very considerably. Each of the two popes drew his strength from the kings who recognized him and backed him; far from being able to order kings about, they were dependent on their good will. The withdrawal of French obedience shows it despite 'Benedict XIII's' magnificently intransigent stand for the totality of the unassailable rights of the Vicar of Christ. The kings had the scholars and the public on their side. It was Christian feeling as a whole which supported the Emperor's calling of the Council of Constance—which in turn put an end to the schism on conditions that made the Emperor the pope's superior. At the same time the pope lost all possibility of even pretending to use his henceforward anachronistic powers. 'Benedict XIII' maintained gallantly that the pope could, and he died deserted and alone at Peñiscola.

Conclusion

The whole evolution of the papacy and the Church was influenced by the popes' sixty-seven years' stay at Avignon. It helped both to develop characteristics which were certainly common to contemporary government and society, but which might not have grown so easily elsewhere. The town was of only middling importance when the popes came there; but it was geographically central to Christendom. Because of both facts the papacy could enjoy a hitherto unknown peace and stability. The curia became sedentary; consequently it became more organized and bureaucratic; consequently also the Church could be more centralized and the pope's authority could be exercised more directly, as was shown by much more regular taxation and the reservation of the vast majority of important benefices to the pope's own appointment. Papal patronage grew, so did a sense of prestige and monarchy, and of wealth to be disposed of. Yet at the same time Avignon favoured the discreet abandonment of papal pretensions to govern all Christians, which would have been harder to forget at Rome. The international Church went through a particularly difficult stage at this period, when Western Christian society ceased to be a congeries of badly co-ordinated principalities, all prepared to defer to the pope at Rome, and became instead a group of great kingdoms in each of which royal authority was increasingly absolute and unwilling to admit any rival. By a parallel evolution the pope's own power became stronger and more centralized, but the very developments which made the papacy stronger in the Church made it weaker in individual kingdoms

Conclusion

where the popes' power over the national churches tended to be reduced by nationalism, and by the growth of an educated laity with strong national feelings. Although kings and popes had similar ambitions, the very structure of the Church meant that these would conflict: royal centralization would conflict with papal centralization. This opposition explains in particular the violent quarrels with the king of France, at once the most powerful king in the West, and the king furthest advanced towards absolutism. The fact that the papacy was at Avignon, at the gates of France, and that the majority of Avignon popes were Frenchmen, meant that compromise was easier, and, before the age of concordats, both facts helped the avoidance of the appalling conflicts which Philip the Fair's quarrel with Boniface VIII had seemed to foreshadow. Thanks to Avignon, papal-French relations were peaceful, and it was even with the help and assistance of the French king that the Church was transformed into a papal monarchy.

The Church is a spiritual society; but it is also a temporal society, and, as such, it evolved just like contemporary states. In the fourteenth century this evolution seemed to many pious people to involve it more than ever before in temporal affairs. There was no great success, like a victorious crusade or a reunion of the Churches, to offset this feeling. The national divisions of Europe prevented the popes from being able to form any common front of Latin Christians against Saracens or schismatics. The pope's hold over Christendom weakened while his power grew in the Church. Since the popes could display no spectacular success, men saw the new structure which they were giving the Church simply as a complication of abuses: nepotism, curial luxury, the heaping up of benefices and a preoccupation with money, all of them things which plainly required reform. The Avignon popes were lawyers, not theologians, and they built up their new administration without paying too much attention to the great surge of mystical devotion produced by the disasters of the fourteenth century and the rise of an educated laity. It seemed doubtful whether they could use their heightened power to make the hierarchy a more spiritualized body of men who lived in greater conformity with the Gospel.

It was just when these questions seemed particularly pressing and acute that the schism broke. There is no doubt whatsoever that the existence of an alternative papal capital and administration at Avignon both helped to cause and prolong the schism. The schism put everything in question, for the laity not only spoke their minds and used their authority, but it was they who compelled the final solution and the whole structure of the Church and the life of the clergy were deeply affected. None the less the work of the Avignon popes endured. Without their solid achievement the fifteenth-century popes could not have lived as they did. Martin V, Eugenius IV and their successors were able to live in the Vatican as their predecessors had lived in the papal palace at Avignon—like them, surrounded by a brilliant, populous court, provided with an efficient bureaucracy, governing an undivided Church and with wealth and a tradition of patronage which allowed them to summon the greatest artists, scholars and humanists to Rome, and to make it a centre of art and learning. The sedentariness and centralization of the Church, the patronage and style of life which were developed at Avignon reappeared at Rome and made up the style of life and government of the Renaissance popes. The problem still was whether these popes would realize the moral and spiritual reform of the Church which the Avignon popes had failed to undertake, a problem which became more urgent the longer it was left, especially in a situation where the education of the laity had been immeasurably advanced by the invention of printing. In the fourteenth century, residence at Avignon had allowed the fourteenth-century popes to create a constitution and administration for the Church which adapted it to new social conditions. It remained for the fifteenth-century popes to adapt it spiritually and morally.

APPENDIX

List of Popes, 1288–1431

The dates of election (=e.), coronation (=c.) and death (=d.) are taken from the *Handbook of Dates for Students of English History*, ed. C. R. Cheney (London, 1961). The date of birth (=b.) and other biographical data are mainly taken from the *New Catholic Encyclopaedia*.

The Roman succession is normally regarded as the legitimate succession. When the Roman pope Gregory XII resigned at Constance, he did so on condition that he reserved the question of the lawfulness of his pontificate. 'By consenting to this, the synod indirectly acknowledged that its previous sessions had not possessed an ecumenical character, and also that Gregory's predecessors, up to Urban VI, had been legitimate popes' (L. Pastor, 'Papacy', *Encyclopaedia Britannica*, 11th ed. (1911), Vol. 20, 704). 'Since 1947 the Vatican *Annuario Pontificio* has printed Mercati's list of popes, which includes 37 antipopes in the text . . . Nicholas V (1328–30), Clement VII (1378–94), Benedict XIII (1394–1423), Alexander V (1409–10), John XXIII (1410–15), Felix V (1439–49) . . . W. Ullmann, *The Origins of the Great Schism* (London, 1948), and Fliche-Martin, 14 (1962), 3–17, provide grounds for considering the Roman succession as the true papal line after 1378' (H. J. Beck, 'Antipope', *New Catholic Encyclopaedia* (1967), Vol. 1, 632–3). The names of Nicholas V, Clement VII, Benedict XIII and John XXIII have all been taken by subsequent popes. Alexander VI, however, did not take the name of Alexander V. It has seemed best to use inverted commas for the names of those antipopes whose names have subsequently been used, in order to avoid possible confusion.

Nicholas IV, Jerome Maschi, Master-General of the Franciscans, b. at Ascolii Piceno in the papal states, September 30th, 1227, e. February 15th/22nd, 1288, c. February 22nd, 1288, d. April 4th, 1292.

St. Celestine V, Peter of Morrone, a Neopolitan hermit, b. at Isernia in south Italy, *circa* 1215, e. July 5th, 1294, c. August 29th, 1294, resigned December 13th, 1294, d. May 19th, 1296.

Boniface VIII, Benedict Gaetani, a Roman nobleman related to Popes Alexander IV and Gregory IX, b. at Anagni in the papal states, *circa* 1235, e. December 24th, 1294, c. January 23rd, 1295, d. October 12th, 1303.

List of Popes, 1288–1431

Blessed Benedict XI, Nicholas Boccasini, a Dominican, b. at Treviso in the Veneto, 1240, e. October 22nd, 1303, c. October 27th, 1303, d. July 7th, 1304.

Clement V, Bertrand de Got, archbishop of Bordeaux, b. at Villandraut in the Garonne, 1264, e. June 5th, 1305, c. November 14th, 1305, d. April 20th, 1314.

John XXII, Jacques Duèse, b. at Cahors in Quercy, 1244, e. August 7th, 1316, c. September 5th, 1316, d. December 4th, 1334.

'Nicholas V', antipope, Pietro Rainalducci, b. at Corvaro (Rieti) in the papal states, a 'Spiritual' Franciscan appointed pope by the Emperor Lewis of Bavaria, e. May 12th, 1328, c. May 22nd, 1328, resigned July 25th, 1330, d. at Avignon October 16th, 1333.

Benedict XII, Jacques Fournier, a Cistercian, b. at Saverdun in the county of Foix, 1285, e. December 20th, 1334, c. January 8th, 1335, d. April 25th, 1342.

Clement VI, Pierre Roger, a Benedictine, b. at Rosier d'Egletons (Maumont) in Guienne, *circa* 1290/1, e. May 7th, 1342, c. May 19th, 1342, d. December 6th, 1352.

Innocent VI, Etienne Aubert, b. at Beyssac in the Limousin, *circa* 1295, e. December 18th, 1352, c. December 30th, 1352, d. September 12th, 1362.

Blessed Urban V, Guillaume de Grimoard, a Benedictine, b. at Grisac in the Gévaudan, *circa* 1318, e. September 28th, 1362, c. November 6th, 1362, d. December 19th, 1370.

Gregory XI, Pierre Roger de Beaufort, nephew of Clement VI, b. at Rosier d'Egletons (Maumont) in Guienne, 1329, e. December 30th, 1370, c. January 5th, 1371, d. March 27th, 1378.

Urban VI, Bartolommeo Prignano, archbishop of Bari, b. at Naples, *circa* 1318, e. April 8th, 1378, c. April 18th, 1378, d. October 15th, 1389.

'Clement VII', antipope, Robert of Geneva, b. at Geneva, 1342, e. at Fondi September 20th, 1378, c. October 31st, 1378, d. September 16, 1394.

Boniface IX, Pietro Tomacelli, b. at Naples, *circa* 1355, e. November 2nd, 1389, c. November 9th, 1389, d. October 1st, 1404.

Innocent VII, Cosmo Megliorati, b. at Sulmona in the kingdom of 'Sicily', e. October 17th, 1404, c. November 11th, 1404, d. November 6th, 1404.

'Benedict XIII', antipope, Pedro de Luna, b. at Illueca in Aragon, *circa* 1328, e. December 28th, 1394, c. October 11th, 1394, deposed by the Council of Pisa, June 5th, 1409,

Gregory XII, Angelo Correr, b. at Venice, *circa* 1325, e. November 30th, 1406, deposed by the Council of Pisa, June 5th, 1409, resigned July 4th, 1415, d. October 18th, 1417.

deposed by the Council of Constance, July 26th, 1417, d. November 29th, 1422.

'*Alexander V*', antipope, Peter Philargus, b. at Candia in Crete, *circa* 1340, Cardinal of the Roman obedience, e. at Pisa, June 26th, 1409, c. July 7th, 1409, d. May 3rd, 1410.

'*John XXIII*', antipope, Baldassare Cossa, b. at Naples, e. May 17th, 1410, c. May 25th, 1410, deposed by the Council of Constance May 29th, 1415, d. November 22nd, 1419.

'*Clement VIII*', antipope, Gil Munoz, e. at Peniscola to succeed 'Benedict XIII', June 10th, 1423, only recognized in the county of Armagnac, resigned July 26th, 1429.

Martin V, Odo Colonna, a Roman nobleman, b. at Genazzano, 1368, e. at Constance November 11th, 1417, c. November 21st, 1417, d. February 20th, 1431.

Bibliography

1. Brief Bibliography

The principal documents concerning the Avignon popes which have been published are:

(a) Papal letters:

Regestum Clementis Papae V, edited by the Benedictines of Monte Cassino, 1884–92, 8 vols.

Letters, Close, Secret and Patent, published as complete texts for the popes subsequent to Clement V.

Litterae Communes (letters written to a standard set form), brought out in a calendar form as short summaries written in French.

Both are being published by the members of the French School at Rome and the chaplains of the church of St. Louis des Français in Rome. 22 volumes have so far appeared.

(b) Papal accounts:

Die Einnahmen and *Die Ausgaben der apostolischen Kammer*, published in a digested form by the members of the Görres-Gesellschaft in the series *Vatikanische Quellen zur Geschichte der paepstlichen Hof- und Finanzverwaltung (1316–1378)*. 7 vols. have so far appeared, (1–6, Paderborn, 1910–37; 7, ed. M. Hoberg, 1944).

(c) Chronicles relating to the popes' lives and pontificates:

Vitae Paparum Avionensium (1305–1394), put together and edited by Baluze in 1693; re-edited with notes by G. Mollat, 4 vols. (Paris, 1916–22).

Bibliography

On the various principal aspects of the Avignon papacy see:

E. Delaruelle, 'Avignon capitale', *Revue géographique des Pyrénées et du Sud-Ouest*, Vol. 23 (1952), 233–64.

L.-H. Labande, *Le palais des Papes et les monuments d'Avignon au XIVe siecle* (Aix/Marseilles, 1925), 2 vols.

G. Mollat, *La collation des bénéfices ecclésiastiques par les Papes d'Avignon (1305–1378)* (Paris, 1921).

B. Guillemain, *La politique bénéficiale du pape Benoit XII* (Paris, 1952).

G. Mollat and Ch. Samaran, *La fiscalité pontificale en France au XIVe siecle* (Paris, 1905).

Y. Renouard, *Les relations des Papes et des Compagnies commerciales et bancaires de 1316 à 1378* (Paris, 1941).

E. Dupré-Theseider, *I papi di Avignone e la questione romana* (Florence, 1939).

Noël Valois, *La France et le Grand Schisme d'Occident* Paris, 1896–1902), 4 vols.

A. Coville, *La vie intellectuelle dans les domaines d'Anjou-Provence de 1380 à 1435* (Paris, 1941).

Ch. Sterling, *Les peintres du Moyen Age*, 2nd ed. (Paris, 1950).

Georges de Lagarde, *La naissance de l'esprit laïque au declin du Moyen Age* (Saint-Paul Trois Châteaux and Paris, 1934–46), 6 vols.

Marguerite Roques, *Les peintures murales du Sud-Est de la France (XIIIe–XVIe siècle)* (Paris, 1961).

But for the period before the schism the fundamental and classic work is by G. Mollat, *Les Papes d'Avignon (1305–1378)*. It should be consulted in the 9th edition (Paris, 1949) (see also p. 141 for English translation (London, 1963)), which contains a full and exhaustive bibliography up to that date. It is the fullest and most systematic treatment of the subject.

Bibliography

2. ADDITIONAL BIBLIOGRAPHY FOR ENGLISH EDITION

A. *Sources*

The great work of the French School at Rome still continues and is near completion. They have, moreover, published indexes to the Register of Pope Clement V (1957) (see reviews by J. R. L. Highfield, *English Historical Review*, 70 (1955), 479; 72 (1957), 361; 73 (1958), 145, 517; 75 (1960), 337; 76 (1961), 134, 352; 78 (1963), 159; 79 (1964), 585; 80 (1965), 820; 82 (1967), 599).

The Public Record Office in London has published a calendar in English of entries in the papal registers relating to Great Britain by W. H. Bliss: *Petitions*, Vol. 1 (1342–1419) (London, 1896); *Papal Letters*, Vol. 2 (1305–42), Vol. 3 (1342–62), Vol. 4 (1362–1404) (London, 1895–1962). These cover periods not yet covered by the French School and should, where possible, be compared with their work.

B. *Secondary Works*

The promised volume of Fliche and Martin's great history of the Church, which will cover the period of the Avignon papacy, has not yet appeared; but that covering the schism and the Conciliar Movement now has:

E. Delaruelle, E.-H. Labande and P. Ourliac, *L'Eglise au temps du Grande Schisme et de la crise conciliaire, 1378–1449*, Histoire de l'Eglise, ed. A. Fliche and V. Martin, Vol. 14 (2 vols.) (Paris, 1962).

The other two important works which have appeared since Professor Renouard wrote are:

B. Guillemain, *La cour pontificale d'Avignon, 1309–1376, etude d'une société* (Paris, 1962).
J. Favier, *Les finances pontificales à l'époque du Grande Schisme d'Occident, 1378–1409* (Paris, 1966).

Bibliography

All three of these contain very full bibliographies.

A survey of literature as it appears will be found—conveniently arranged under themes and pontificates—in *Archivum Historiae Pontificiae* (Vol. 1, Rome, 1963: continuing).

C. *Reading List of Works in English*

I. *General Treatments*

First, and most important, Canon Mollat's history of the Avignon popes has been translated into English by Janet Love: *The Popes at Avignon, 1305–1378* (London, 1963). A good, brief, non-Catholic history of the medieval papacy has just appeared by G. Barraclough: *The Medieval Papacy* (London, 1968). Old, but still brilliantly readable, is M. Creighton, *A History of the Papacy from the Great Schism to the Sack of Rome* (2nd ed., London, 1903–5).

II. *Constitutional History and Political Theory*

A good recent review will be found in *Europe in the Middle Ages*, ed. J. R. Hale, J. R. L. Highfield and B. Smalley (London, 1965): B. Smalley, 'Church and State, 1300–77: Theory and Fact', 15–44. An account of the debates over papal power will be found in A. J. and R. W. Carlyle, *Medieval Political Theory in the West*, Vol. 5 (Edinburgh, 1928).

See also:

W. Ullmann, *Medieval Papalism. The Political Theories of the Medieval Canonists* (London, 1949).

A. Gwynn, *The English Austin Friars in the Time of Wyclif* (London, 1940): a much more wide-ranging account of the period than its title might perhaps suggest.

M. J. Wilks, *The Problem of Sovereignty in the Middle Ages* (Cambridge, 1963).

W. Ullmann, 'The development of the medieval idea of sovereignty', *English Historical Review*, Vol. 64 (1949), 7–33

For the troubles of Boniface VIII, see:

T. S. R. Boase, *Boniface VIII* (London, 1933): very difficult to obtain and urgently requires reprinting.

Bibliography

F. M. Powicke, 'Boniface VIII', *Christian Life in the Middle Ages* (Oxford, 1935), 48–74.

A brief collection of conflicting interpretations is excerpted in:
Philip the Fair and Boniface VIII, ed. C. T. Wood (New York, 1967).
J. B. Strayer, 'Philip the Fair' a constitutional king', *American Historical Review*, Vol. 62 (1956–7), 18–32.

For the papacy's troubles with the Empire, see:
W. M. Bowsky, *Henry VII in Italy* (Lincoln, Nebraska, 1960).
W. M. Bowsky, 'Florence and Henry of Luxemburg', *Speculum*, Vol. 33 (1958), 177–204.
W. M. Bowsky, 'Clement V and the Emperor elect', *Medievalia et Humanistica*, Vol. 12 (1958), 52–70.
W. M. Bowsky, 'Dante's Italy, a political dissection', *The Historian*, Vol. 21 (1958), 82–100.
H. S. Offler, 'Empire and papacy, the last struggle', *Transactions of the Royal Historical Society*, 5th series, Vol. 6 (1956), 177–203.
C. C. Bayley, *The Formation of the German College of Electors* (Toronto, 1949).

Under this heading a separate bibliography could be given to Dante for whose views (briefly) see:
A. P. d'Entrèves, *Dante as a Political Thinker* (Oxford, 1952).
C. T. Davis, *Dante and the Idea of Rome* (Oxford, 1957).
Dante's Monarchy and Three Political Letters, trans. D. Nicholl and C. Hardie (London, 1954).

For the papacy's troubles with the Franciscans, see:
M. D. Lambert, *Franciscan Poverty* (London, 1961).
Decima L. Douie, *The Nature and Effect of the Heresy of the Fraticelli* (Manchester, 1932).
J. R. H. Moorman, *The History of the Franciscan Order from its Origins to the year 1517* (Oxford, 1968).

For the 'secular' theorists and the papacy, see:
N. Rubinstein, 'Marsilius of Padua and the Italian political

theorists of his time', Hale, Highfield and Smalley, op. cit., 44–76.

C. W. Previté-Orton, 'Marsilius of Padua', *Proceedings of the British Academy*, Vol. 21 (1935).

Marsiglio's writings have been translated by A. Gewirth, *Marsilius of Padua* (New York, 1951–6).

For the constitutional and theoretical movements which led up to the Great Schism, see:

W. Ullmann, *The Origins of the Great Schism* (London, 1948).

For the Conciliar Movement, see:

B. Tierney, *The Foundations of Conciliar Theory* (Cambridge, 1966).

E. F. Jacob, *Essays in the Conciliar Epoch*, 2nd ed. (Manchester, 1953).

J. B. Morrall, *Gerson and the Great Schism* (Manchester, 1960).

P. E. Sigmund, *Nicholas of Cusa* (Cambridge, Mass., 1961).

J. P. Macgovern, *Pierre d'Ailly* (Washington, D.C., 1936).

L. R. Loomis, 'Nationality at the Council of Constance', *American Historical Review*, Vol. 44 (1939), 508–27.

For the gradual increase of power over the Church in the national monarchies, the best example is perhaps England: see below.

III. *The Papal State and Italy*

Unfortunately there is no good book in English on the papal state in the fourteenth century, but see:

D. P. Waley, *The Papal State in the Thirteenth Century* (London, 1961).

P. Partner, *The Papal State under Martin V* (London, 1958).

John Larner, *The Lords of the Romagna* (London, 1965).

D. P. Waley, 'An account book of the patrimony of St. Peter in Tuscany 1304–1305', *Journal of Ecclesiastical History*, Vol. 6 (1955), 18–25.

P. J. Jones, 'The Vicariate of the Malatesta of Rimini', *English Historical Review*, Vol. 67 (1952), 321–51.

Bibliography

For the state of Rome, see:

F. Gregorovius, *A History of the City of Rome in the Middle Ages* (London, 1894–1902).

For the political background in Italy, see:

D. P. Waley, *Europe in the Later Middle Ages* (London, 1964).

P. J. Jones, 'Communes and despots: the city state in late medieval Italy', *Transactions of the Royal Historical Society*, 5th series, Vol. 15 (1965), 71–97.

P. Partner, 'Florence and the papacy 1300–1375', Hale, Highfield and Smalley, op. cit., 76–122.

M. V. Becker, 'Some economic implications of the conflict between Church and state in "trecento" Florence', *Medieval Studies*, Vol. 21 (1959), 1–6.

For the Visconti, see:

D. M. Bueno de Mesquita, *Giangaleazzo Visconti, 1351–1402* (Cambridge, 1941).

IV. *Papal Finance and Administration*

An excellent brief introduction to papal taxation will be found in:

K. J. Scarisbrick, 'Clerical taxation in England 1485–1547', *Journal of Ecclesiastical History*, Vol. 11 (1960), 41–54; and

P. Partner, 'Camera Papae, problems of papal finance in the later middle ages', ibid., Vol. 4 (1953), 55–68.

W. E. Lunt, *Papal Revenues in the Middle Ages* (New York, 1934), provides illustrative documents with commentary.

The standard work on papal provisions is:

G. Barraclough, *Papal Provisions* (Oxford, 1935).

See also the comments of:

W. A. Pantin, *The English Church in the Fourteenth Century* (Cambridge, 1955).

And finally:

G. Barraclough, *Public Notaries and the Papal Curia* (London, 1934).

V. *Religion and the Church at Large*

No topic has been so generally neglected as religious history as such, and scholars writing in English have concentrated on the three topics of Saints, Mystics and Heresy.

(i) Saints:

Of many lives of Catherine of Siena a recent scholarly one is A. Levasti, *My Servant Catherine,* trans. by D. M. White (Westminster, Maryland, 1954). The contemporary life by Blessed Raymond of Capua has been translated by D. M. Lamb (London, 1960); her letters by V. D. Scudder (London, 1905); and her Dialogue, with a contemporary account of her death, by A. Thorold (London, 1925). For St. Brigid of Sweden, see the life by J. Jorgensen, trans. by Ingeborg Lund, 2 vols. (London, 1954).

(ii) Mystics:

E. Gebhardt, *Mystics and Heretics in Italy,* trans. E. M. Hulme (London, 1922).

D. Knowles, *The English Mystical Tradition* (London, 1967).

J. M. Clark, *The Great German Mystics* (Oxford, 1949).

(iii) Heretics:

G. Leff, *Heresy in the Later Middle Ages,* 2 vols. (Manchester, 1967).

M. Reeves, *The Influence of Prophecy in the Later Middle Ages: A Study in Joachimism* (Oxford, 1969).

N. Cohn, *The Pursuit of the Millenium* (London, 1962); see also the forthcoming book by M. D. Lambert.

J. G. Sikes, 'John de Pouilly and Peter de la Palu', *English Historical Review,* Vol. 49 (1934), 219–40.

On the popes and education, see:

L. E. Boyle, 'The constitution "cum ex eo" of Boniface VIII', *Medieval Studies,* Vol. 24 (1962), 263–302.

'The curriculum of the faculty of canon law at Oxford in the first half of the fourteenth century', *Oxford Studies Presented to Daniel Callus* (Oxford Historical Society, 1964), 150–60.

Bibliography

On missions, see *The Mongol Mission; Narratives and Letters of the Franciscan Missionaries in Mongolia and China in the Thirteenth and Fourteenth Centuries*, ed. C. Dawson (London, 1961).

VI. *England and the Papacy*

The whole course of Anglo-papal relations in the Middle Ages has recently been surveyed in a volume of essays, *The English Church and the Papacy in the Middle Ages*, ed. C. H. Lawrence (London, 1965): see 'The thirteenth century' (C. H. Lawrence, 117–57), 'The fourteenth century' (W. A. Pantin, 157–95), 'The fifteenth century' (F. R. H. Du Boulay, 195–243). W. A. Pantin has as well surveyed the subject (and scarcely repeats himself) in his *The English Church in the Fourteenth Century* (Cambridge, 1955), which also provides the best account of what it was like to be a Christian in England in the fourteenth century. See also:

E. Bishop, 'Nova et vetera: how English Catholics prayed in the fourteenth century', *Dublin Review*, October, 1898, 391–401.

E. Bishop, 'On the social status of the English clergy in the fourteenth and fifteenth centuries', *The New Era*, December 16th, 1899, 5.

G. R. Owst, *Preaching in Medieval England* (Cambridge, 1926).

G. R. Owst, *Literature and the Pulpit in Medieval England* (Cambridge, 1933).

B. L. Manning, *The People's Faith in the Time of Wycliffe* (Oxford, 1919).

A. Hamilton Thompson, *The English Clergy and their Organization in the Later Middle Ages* (Oxford, 1947).

R. Brentano, *York Metropolitan Jurisdiction and Papal Judges Delegate* (Berkeley, Cal., 1959).

On the financial relations, see:

W. E. Lunt, *Financial Relations of the Papacy with England 1327–1534* (Medieval Academy of America, publication no. 74, Cambridge, Mass., 1962).

On the way in which the national monarchy assumed control

Bibliography

of the Church, a most important article is J. R. L. Highfield's 'The English hierarchy in the reign of Edward III',
Transactions of the Royal Historical Society, 5th series, Vol. 6
(1956), 115–39. This should be compared with K. Edwards's
'The political importance of the English bishops during the
reign of Edward II', *English Historical Review*, Vol. 59 (1944),
311–47, and 'The Social origins and provenance of the English
bishops during the reign of Edward II', *Transactions of the Royal
Historical Society*, 5th series, Vol. 9 (1959), 51–79 (see also the
general remarks of M. D. Knowles, 'The English bishops 1070–
1532', *Medieval Studies Presented to Aubrey Gwynn, S.J.* (Dublin,
1961), 283–97). On increasing royal control, see also G. L.
Harriss, 'Medieval government and statecraft', *Past and Present*,
no. 25 (1963), 8–39.

On anti-papal legislation, see:

Cecily Davies, 'The Statute of Provisors of 1351', *History*, new series, Vol. 38 (1953), 116–33.

W. T. Waugh, 'The Great Statute of Praemunire, 1393', *English Historical Review*, Vol. 37 (1922), 173–205.

E. G. Graves, 'The legal significance of the statute of praemunire of 1353', *Haskins Anniversary Essays* (Boston, New York, 1929), and his report on research on the judicial relations of the papacy with England in *Year Book of the American Philosophical Society* (1954).

For royal seizure of Church property, see:

M. M. Morgan, 'The suppression of the alien priories', *History*, new series, Vol. 26 (1941/2).

On papal provision and its effects, see:

A. Deeley, 'Papal provision and royal rights of patronage in the early fourteenth century', *English Historical Review*, Vol. 43 (1928), 497–527.

E. F. Jacob, 'Petitions for benefices from English clerks during the Great Schism', *Transactions of the Royal Historical Society*, 4th series, Vol. 37 (1945), 41–59, and 'On the promotion of

Bibliography

English university clerks during the later Middle Ages',
Journal of Ecclesiastical History, Vol. 1 (1950), 172–86.

On Wycliffe and the Lollards a long bibliography would be possible. Despite his acid lack of sympathy and his under-valuing of later Lollardry, the best introduction and a brilliant book in itself is K. B. Macfarlane's *John Wycliffe and the Beginnings of English Nonconformity* (London, 1952). See also M. D. Knowles, *The Religious Orders in England*, Vol. II (Cambridge, 1957), and 'The censured opinions of Uthred of Boldon', *Proceedings of the British Academy*, Vol. 37 (1951), 305–42.

For Pope Clement V's background as a clerk in the service of Edward I, see J. H. Denton, 'Pope Clement V's career as a royal clerk', *English Historical Review*, Vol. 83 (1968), 303–14. For an English view of the schism, see L. Macfarlane, 'An English account of the election of Urban VI', *Bulletin of the Institute of Historical Research*, Vol. 26 (1953), 75–85. See also W. Ullmann, 'Cambridge and the Great Schism', *Journal of Theological Studies*, new series, Vol. 9 (1958), 53–77.

VII. *Ireland and the Papacy*

The most recent review of the period will be found in A. Gwynn, 'Anglo-Irish Church Life in the fourteenth and fifteenth centuries', *A History of Irish Catholicism*, ed. P. J. Corish (Dublin, 1968).

See also:

- Sr. M. Angela Bolster, 'The diocese of Cork and the great Western schism', *Journal of the Cork Historical and Archaeological Society*, Vol. 71 (1966), 92–102.
- A. Gwynn, 'Ireland and the English nation at the Council of Constance', *Proceedings of the Royal Irish Academy*, Vol. 45 (1940), Section C, 183–233.
- A. Gwynn and D. F. Gleeson, *A History of the Diocese of Killaloe* (Dublin, 1962).
- J. Watt, 'Negotiations between Edward II and John XXII concerning Ireland', *Irish Historical Studies*, Vol. 10 (1956), 1–20.

148

Bibliography

U. Flanagan, 'Papal provisions in Ireland 1307–1378', *Historical Studies*, Vol. 3 (1961), 92–103.

VIII. *General Political Background*

Among a number of general histories are M. H. Keen, *A History of Medieval Europe* (London, 1968), and D. Hay, *Europe in the Fourteenth and Fifteenth Centuries* (London, 1966). A recent survey of the Hundred Years' War with a very full bibliography is K. Fowler, *The Age of Plantagenet and Valois* (London, 1967). An account in English of some of the papal peace negotiations is H. Jenkins, *Papal Efforts for Peace under Benedict XII* (Philadelphia, 1933). On the crusade, see A. Luttrell, 'The crusade in the fourteenth century', Hale, Highfield and Smalley, op. cit., 122–55. A useful book, giving views for negotiations over the schism is P. E. Russell, *The English Intervention in Spain and Portugal in the Time of Edward III and Richard II* (Oxford, 1955).

IX. *Avignon Itself*

Virtually nothing written in English exists. There is an old guide in the Medieval Towns Series: *The Story of Avignon* by T. Okey (London, 1911); and there is a recent life of a great cardinal of the period by P. N. Zacour: 'Talleyrand, the cardinal of Perigord (1301–1364)', *Transactions of the American Philosophical Society*, new series, Vol. 50, part 7 (Philadelphia, 1960); and another of a Carmelite diplomat and martyr by F. J. Boehlke: *Pierre de Thomas, Scholar, Diplomat and Crusader* (Philadelphia, 1966). For what it was like to be an Italian merchant living in Avignon, see I. Origo's delightful *The Merchant of Prato* (London, 1957).

X. *The Arts and Literature*

On Petrarch, certainly the greatest writer who lived at Avignon, see Morris Bishop, *Petrarch and his World* (Indiana, 1963), E. H. Wilkins, *Studies in the Life and Work of Petrarch* (Chicago, 1961), and J. H. Whitfield, *Petrarch and the Renaissance* (Oxford, 1943). Petrarch's *Letters* have been translated in selection by M. Bishop (Indiana, 1966), *The Life of Solitude* by J. Zeitlin

(Urbana, 1924), the *Secret* by W. H. Draper (London, 1911), and the *Letters to Classical Authors* by M. E. Cosenza (Chicago, 1910).

On 'humanism', see R. Weiss, *The Dawn of Humanism in Italy* (London, 1947), B. L. Ullmann, *The Humanism of Coluccio Salutati* (Padua, 1963), and *The Origin and Development of the Humanistic Script* (Rome, 1960). On classicizing at Avignon and for a brilliant discussion of fourteenth century 'renaissance' in Northern lands, see B. Smalley, *The English Friars and Antiquity in the Later Middle Ages* (Oxford, 1960).

On the arts there is again very little in English: Sylvain Gagniere, *The Palace of the Popes at Avignon* (Nancy and Paris, 1965), and A. K. Mann, *Tombs and Portraits of the Popes of the Middle Ages* (London, 1928).

The following important books have appeared since Renouard wrote:

M. Laclotte, *L'Ecole d'Avignon* (Paris, 1960).
Enrico Castelnuovo, *Un pittore italiano alla corte di Avignone, Matteo Giovanetti e la pittura in Provenza nel secolo XIV* (Turin, 1962).

On contemporary art in Italy, see:

John White, *Art and Architecture in Italy 1250–1400* (London, 1966).
Millard Meiss, *Painting in Florence and Siena after the Black Death* (Princeton, 1951).

Index

Index

Index

Colonna family, 13, 14, 17, 18, 29, 40, 45

commendation, 99

Comtat Venaissin, 17, 21-2, 47, 65, 82-3

Constance, Council of, 78, 108, 131

Constantinople, 32, 57, 60, 117

Constitutions of Albornoz, 50-1

Corneto, 59, 61, 66

corruption in papal court, 28, 118

Council, General: 106, 108, 117, 121, 122; Boniface VIII called before, 13, 18; of Basel, 78, 108; of Constance, 108, 131; of Pisa, 107, 108; of Lyons, 37; of Vienne, 21, 22, 24, 29, 107, 108, 124

Cracow, 32-4

Crécy, battle of, 43

Cros, Pierre de, 72

crusades: tithes for, 14, 29, 101, 103, 118; importance to Church's authority, 15, 18, 96, 116, 117; plans by popes for, 29, 30, 35, 39, 43, 48, 49, 56-7, 60, 62-4; of count of Nevers, 77-8; of 1340, 50

Cuença, 49

Cyprus, 43, 69, 71

Defensor Pacis, 126

Dominicans, 120

Duèse, Jacques. *See* John XXII

Durançole, river, 81

Durand, Guillaume, 117

Durfort, Astorge de, 44, 48

Eckhart, 120

Edinburgh, 32-4

Edward I of England, 18, 20

Edward II of England, 21

Edward III of England, 30, 40, 61, 64, 65, 128-9, 131

Edward the Black Prince, 49, 61

Egypt, 64

Eight Saints, War of, 64

England: position in schism, 69; papal suzerainty over, 128-9; *see also* Aquitaine, Hundred Years War.

Eugenius IV, pope, 108, 134

Fano, Constitutions of, 51

Fécamp, 42

Felix Societas Balestriorum et Pavesatorum, 58

Ferrara, 21, 28

Fidate, Simone, 120

Flagellants, 120

Flanders, 69

Florence, 29, 63-6, 77; merchant banks of, 36, 44, 93, 104, 129

Fontfroide, 38

Fortunate Islands, 130

Fournier, Jacques: *see* Benedict XII

France: royal succession in, 39; position in schism, 69, 71, 73, 78; *see also* Aquitaine, Hundred Years War

Franciscans, 13, 118, 119, 126; *see also* Fraticelli

Fraticelli, 38, 119

Frederick of Austria, 30, 125

Frederick of Trinacria, 39, 40

Fréjus, 28

friars, mendicant, 14, 105, 120

Gaetani family, 14, 17, 29

Gallipoli, 56

Gasbert of Laval, 100, 102, 104, 105

Geneva, 71

Genoa, 66

Ghibelline alliance, 29-31, 39, 45, 126

Golden Rose, 89

Got, Bertrand de: *see* Clement V

Greece, 77

Greek schism, 32, 60, 62

Gregory VII, pope, 14, 96, 97, 106, 116, 117, 123

Gregory X, pope, 37, 62

Gregory XI, pope, 61-6, 71, 73, 74, 88, 99, 111, 113

Grimoard, Anglic de, 55

Grimoard, Guillaume de: *see* Urban V

Groseau, 24

Index

Raymond VII, count of Toulouse, 22

reform of Church needed, 117, 118, 120–2, 133, 134

Rhense, Declaration of, 127

Rhône valley, 34–5

Rienzo, Cola di, 45, 46, 68

Rieti, 82

Robert of Geneva, cardinal, 65, 69; see also 'Clement VII'

Robert of Anjou, count of Provence, king of 'Sicily', 28–30, 39, 44, 125

Roche, Androin de la, 51, 88

Roger, Pierre: see Clement VI

Romagna, 17, 28–30, 39, 44, 50, 51, 63

Rome: disturbances in, 17, 29, 30, 37, 40, 45, 46; position of in Christian world, 32, 47, 48, 57, 62, 63; communications with, 35; climate of, 82; St. Peter's, 40, 60; Lateran Palace, 59; Vatican, 59; papal vicar in, 29; Urban V returns to, 58–61; Gregory XI moves to, 65, 66; election of Urban VI, 66–9; during the schism, 70–1, 78

Roquemaure, 24

Rouen, 42

Ruysbroeck, 120

Sachsenhausen, 126

Sacred College: see cardinals

St. Bertrand de Comminges, 20

St. Gilles, 36

St. John, knights of, 43

Salutati, Coluccio, 114

Sarzana, 66

Savoy, 69

Scaligeri, 29

schism: possibility of, 63; beginning of, 69, 107; resolved by Council of Constance, 108, 122; damage done by, 131, 134. See also 'Clement VII', 'Benedict XIII', Greek schism

Scotland, 39, 69

Sens, 42

Sicily, 22 n., 40, 69, 71, 78, 129

Siena, 66

Smyrna, capture of, 43

spoils, 103

Sorgues, 82, 85, 112

Spoleto, duchy of, 17, 50

Stefaneschi, cardinal, 112

Stockholm, 32–4

Suso, 120

Syria, 117

Tarifa, 50

Tauler, 120

Thérouanne, 71

Thomas Aquinas, St., 123

Tibaldeschi, cardinal, 68–9

Toledo, 49

Toulouse, university of, 49, 53 tributes of vassal kingdoms, 102, 128

Trinacria, 22, 29, 39

Turks, 32 n., 57, 77, 117

Tuscany, 28, 29, 62, 63

Ubaldi, Piero Baldi degli, 62, 90

universities, papal influence exerted through, 14, 99, 105, 106

Urban II, pope, 14, 43, 57, 96

Urban IV, pope, 22 n.

Urban V, pope, 53, 55–63, 65, 68, 73, 99, 101, 113, 128

Urban VI, pope, 68–70, 72, 74, 75

vacancies, 103

Vaison, 22

vassalage of kings to the pope, 14, 102, 124, 125, 128

Venice, 21, 28, 35

Verona, 29

Via, cardinal Arnaud de, 112

Via, Jacques de, 25

Vico, Giovanni di, 50

Vienne: 20, 34; Council of, 21, 22, 24, 29, 34, 35, 88, 107, 108, 124

Villeneuve-les-Avignon, 82, 112, 115

Vincennes, assembly at, 42

Visconti family, 28, 29, 50, 63, 66, 127

Index

DATE DUE

11/4			
NO 16 '72			
NOV 3 0 1972			
JE 11 '76			